Directions for
Communication

Directions for Communication

DISCOVERIES WITH
IGNATIUS LOYOLA

Willi Lambert

Translated from the German by
Robert R. Barr, Marlies Parent,
and Peter Heinegg

A Crossroad Book
The Crossroad Publishing Company
New York

The Crossroad Publishing Company
16 Penn Plaza, 481 Eighth Avenue
New York, NY 10001

Originally published under the title *Die Kunst der Kommunikation,*
copyright © 1999 by Verlag Herder, Freiburg im Breisgau

English translation copyright © 2000 by
The Crossroad Publishing Company

Printed in the United States of America

Library of Congress Cataloging-in-Publication Data
Lambert, Willi.
   [Kunst der Kommunikation. English]
   Directions for communication : discoveries with Ignatius Loyola /
Willi Lambert ; translated from the German by Robert R. Barr,
Marlies Parent, and Peter Heinegg.
     p. cm.
   Includes bibliographical references.
   ISBN 0-8245-1853-5 (alk. paper)
   1. Communication – Religious aspects – Catholic Church.
2. Ignatius, of Loyola, Saint, 1491-1556 – Contributions in religious
aspects of communication. I. Title.
BX1795.C67 L3613 2000
248 – dc21
                                                  00-008576

I dedicate this book in a special way to

FATHER PEDRO ARRUPE, S.J.
General of the Jesuits 1965–83
He experienced the atom bomb at Hiroshima
and lived dialogue in a sparkling, vital,
and faith-filled manner.

POPE PAUL VI
He called dialogue a "new manner of being church"
and experienced the need of a dialogue,
in all its harsh difficulties,
that would be open to the world.

BISHOP KARL LEHMANN
President of the German Bishops Conference
He has to sit between two completely different chairs:
rather a Christian place to sit.

ROMAN HERZOG
President of the Federal Republic of Germany (1995–99)
In some of his Christmas addresses, and in many speeches,
he encouraged his hearers to dialogue
and called for communication in a democratic society.

A CONFRERE
He has the gift of offering his friendship
in a chaotic and communicative style.

Contents

Introduction

Did the following story actually happen? Nobody knows, but it seems a good way to start off this book: A man was talking with a Jesuit one day and got tired of the way he always answered a question with a counter-question. "Why do you do that?" the man asked. "Why not?" replied the Jesuit. Of course, that wasn't an answer and only served to underline the way the conversation had gone. We'll never know whether the constant counter-questioning was actually helpful (a sort of midwifery, perhaps) or only pointed up the Jesuit's refusal to take a stand.

Ignatius Loyola: Expert in Communication

However that may be, it does raise the question of communication. Ordinarily, this is not a question people connect with Ignatius Loyola (1491–1556). Ignatius is famous as master of the Exercises. He is famous as founder and first general of the Jesuits, that somewhat "mysterious" order. But Ignatius as an expert in communication? Negative! If you want to embarrass a Jesuit, you need only ask for specifics on Ignatius's "communication skills."

For me personally, as for so many, Ignatius was mainly the man of the "dark night," whom scruples drove to the brink of suicide. He was the man of the Exercises and the founding of the order. But then, a number of years ago, I discovered a certain Ignatian text. That text has become a pivot of my life and work. It is a letter, dispatched in 1546 to three confreres who had been sent to the Council of Trent. On this occasion, Ignatius sends to the conciliar theologians not a catechism, but...rules for communication! This key experience initiated a journey of discovery for me that very soon, and at an accelerating pace, showed me Ignatius as a master of communication.

Communication: Current Fashion?
Sign of the Times? Field of Encounter?

It was both an advantage and a disadvantage on this journey of discovery that there was simply no literature that addressed the subject of Ignatian communication. Where it is touched on obliquely, one sees that the subject of communication is a field in which needs of our time and society can enter into a fruitful relationship with knowledge about communication from the past and with experiences of spiritual tradition. These relations will serve the profit of both partners in the dialogue. The connection between management and spirituality was not a casual matter for Ignatius Loyola, or one of current fad, but was "experienced reality." Were we to expand our journey of discovery right to the linguistic roots of "communication," we should see at once that we need not dig very deep at all. Duden's *Herkunftswörterbuch der deutschen Sprache* (Etymological dictionary of the German language) cites, among other words sharing the same etymology as "communication," *Kommuniqué* (communiqué), *Kommun* (commune), *Kommunismus* (Communism), *Kommunion* (communion), and *Kommunizieren* (to communicate). "Common" has a broad field of denotation: "common to several or to all; usual; to do something together, share information, discuss something, to do something in community." The Latin word *munus*, as well, in the sense of "achievement, office, assignment, checking, registering for safekeeping, gift, favor" is in the connotation, and in the syllable *-mei-* has the meaning of "change, exchange, take turns." The word and concept of "communication" is itself "communicative," in that it is a testimonial to the community of the German-French-English-Spanish-Latin interrelated languages.

Significance of a Discovery

It is scarcely difficult to defend the proposition that discovery of and attention to the communicative dimension of Ignatian spirituality and lifestyle are potentially meaningful for many areas, and in a variety of relationships. They can be:

- Meaningful for a more comprehensive picture of Ignatius and his spirituality.

- Meaningful for all of those stamped by Ignatian spirituality.

- Meaningful for balancing off a certain individualistic inclination that emphasizes one side of Ignatian spirituality — in the name of Ignatius himself.

- Meaningful for the discovery that a concern for communication is not just a fashion of the twentieth century, but is anchored deep in spiritual tradition.

- Meaningful because so many conflictive situations in the church fairly cry out for less wooden ways of communication.

- Meaningful because dialogue can bind the church to the world around it and open its gates wider.

- Meaningful because successful communication is a boon that can render the life of persons joyful, gladsome, and thankful.

- Meaningful because these "discoveries with Ignatius Loyola" could perhaps be a help for life — and this would be the most beautiful meaningfulness of all!

So Important — and Nothing Written about It?

With so many "meaningfuls," it is understandable that one should suspect that, after all, there really must have been a great deal written on the subject of Ignatius and communication. The fact is: next to nothing has been written. Here is just one more in a whole series of "memory lapses" of the Jesuits: Until the current century, *Pilgrim's Report*, a kind of spiritual autobiography of Ignatius, was all but intentionally kept under lock and key. The spiritual diary of Ignatius, as well, gathered dust for a long time. And even the original form of the Ignatian Exercises — which their author produced for pairs of individuals, with one-on-one "direction," or rather accompaniment, of the individual "making" the Exercises — was scarcely practiced any more. Finally, Ignatius himself already practiced the "daily exercises of piety," that is, the Exercises adapted for daily life, which are enjoying a veritable resurrection today and in many communities afford a fruitful contribution to a spiritual renewal. It should come as no surprise that an awareness of Ignatius's great knowledge of communication, as well, has seen little development, and his "communicative competence" has not entered as much as it could have into Jesuit formation, community life, and pastoral theory and practice. If the rediscovery of the Ignatian "art of communication" might bear only half as much good fruit as the rediscovery of the individual Exercises, that would be a "bold stroke of grace."

Some few books in German, dealing expressly — at least in part — with communication and Ignatian spirituality, should be listed briefly here, without, of course, a critical evaluation. Those interested only in "discoveries" can safely omit a reading of the following few pages as less than crucial for that interest.

In 1976, not in print but as a dissertation, Gerard Th. A. Wilkens, S.J., "Unterwegs zum Orden" (On the way to the order) appeared. Its subtitle compendiously expresses the direction taken: "Spiritual Genesis and Development of Interpersonal Relationships in the History of the Founding of the Society of Jesus, and a Theological Evaluation of the Same." Anyone concerned with history, or inclined to pursue lines of growth, or interested in textual testimonials and an "inside view" of the genesis of the order and the communication-community of the Jesuits will here find abundant material, set forth and analyzed.

In 1977, Helmut Stich's *Kernstrukturen menschlicher Begegnung* (Core structures of human encounter) was published. The subtitle, "Ethical Implications of the Psychology of Communication," echoes the principal interest of the book. The author takes results of humanistic psychology and the investigation of communication and mentions Ignatius in five places, on some ten pages. He argues that Ignatius anticipated some features of Carl Rogers' basic principles and notes that connections between Ignatius and questions about the core structures of human encounter might be interesting to both sides.

In 1978, José R. de Rivera's *Kommunikationsstrukturen in den geistlichen Exerzitien des Ignatius von Loyola* (Structures of communication in the Spiritual Exercises of Ignatius Loyola) appeared. This work investigates, in terms of both theory of communication and sociology of knowledge, the practice of the Exercises as a form of communicating conviction, integrating the exercitant into a community of communication with a common religious framework of relationships. Its compressed language shows that this investigative report is for specialists interested in a nonreligious interpretation as the point of departure for spiritual and theological reflections.

In 1997, on the threshold of the third millennium, Helmut Geiselhart's *Das Management-Modell der Jesuiten* (The management model of the Jesuits) appeared. The subtitle, "A Concept of Success for the Twenty-first Century," may have been composed with marketability in mind, but it does express certain things about the quality of Ignatian and Jesuit "organization," which is always closely linked to the process of communication. Astonishingly, as a trainer and counselor for industrial enterprises, he interprets the Jesuit order as a "learning enterprise." He designates Ignatius's Spiritual Exercises as a "source of success," and uninhibitedly, on page after page, invites the reader to biblical meditations that are orientated to the way of the Exercises.

On Our Manner of a "Mixed" Presentation

It may be useful, for the sake of communication between book, reader, and author, to make certain preliminary observations on the specific nature of this book, for the sake of "truth in advertising." Its main purpose is to afford access to the communicative dimension of Ignatian spirituality. This will be done in a way that is not exactly scholarly though I hope it will be informative. The style, language level, and thematic fields of the book will be "mixed": experiences, quotations, sometimes considerations more theological and spiritual, sometimes more practical motivations and indications for practice.

The relatively many, and occasionally extended, quotations of works of Ignatius, not readily available to the "ordinary" reader, are intended to help toward a familiarity with the original text, although this is not always easy in terms of a "feel" for the text. This too can be understood as an induction into and practice of communication across the "abyss of history." Since we frequently quote from a series of works, corresponding abbreviations will be indicated for them. (See the bibliography at the end of the book.)

There is a certain amount of overlapping from chapter to chapter. This has the advantage of offering the passages in question for reading independently of one another and of the series in which they originally occur. What we have here are various directions and fields of the communicative dimension of Ignatian spirituality.

Erich Fromm's *The Art of Loving* begins by making it clear that loving is an art, that is, it is a matter of inspiration and "perspiration," of intuition and effort. Love is *Gabe und Aufgabe,* gift and task; love is *Gunst und Kunst,* favor and art. The case is the same with communication: it calls for inner openness, and for practice, attention, learning by "trial and error." Not for nothing does the title of Ignatius's *chef-d'oeuvre* read *Exercitia Spiritualia* — "Spiritual Exercises."

It will be noticed that in this book the original "enthusiasm" echoes and reigns throughout. Of course, one could also tell many stories and ask to clarify the boundaries of Ignatius's personality and his method of communication. Here and there, such chords will be sounded. Contrast makes the picture clearer.

"Love Consists in ... "

By way of an ending to this beginning, I should like to share, "communicate," a discovery that for me was one of the most beautiful benefits of the writing of this book. I had already drafted a number of chapters when, "coincidentally," I happened upon the Spanish translation of a word in Ignatius's Book of the Exercises. I had often read it as, "Love consists in sharing." In Spanish, the formulation is: "El amor consiste en comunicación," "Love consists in communication"! Joy and encouragement! Naturally, I had wondered again and again, especially in the beginning: Am I not reading something into Ignatius? Are "directions for communication" really so central for him? Now, altogether surprisingly, I could read that "love consists in communication," in "mutual confiding." Happy Holiday! Let the reader feel free to join in the festivities.

Chapter 1

In the School of Life
Biography and Communication

For physics, Albert Einstein's theory of relativity, not his biography, is of interest. For Sigmund Freud's psychology, a knowledge and understanding of the course of his life is more meaningful. And when someone speaks of the art of communication, as does Ignatius Loyola, one is justifiably curious to know how he behaved when involved with human beings — how he communicated and how he learned communication in the school of life.

In Basque: "I've Bought Myself a Cow"

When we speak of "southerners," for example, of Italians, we may think that they were born "communicative." And we do not mean just with their mouths. They speak with their whole bodies, especially their hands. "Verbal and nonverbal communication" are not, for them, foreign terms from the technical lingo of psychologists, but obvious matters of everyday experience. Even with boys and girls we notice that, interviewed on television, they are delighted and pleased and that they ultimately give the whole nation their opinion of something.

Is Ignatius, too, a "southerner," in the sense of someone who has it easy when it comes to speaking and gesticulating? And will this alone make him an expert in communication? This conclusion would be a double "communication sin." First, it readily implies that anyone who speaks communicates, which is not even true for Italians. I recall one who told me spontaneously that speaking would be even more beautiful if everyone did not try to speak at once, but someone would listen. The second sin would lie in lumping all southern nations together when it comes to character and communication. Ignatius the Basque was not an Italian, or even a Spaniard, but precisely a Basque.

When I asked a Basque confrere to give me the key characteristic of a Basque conversation, he told me a story. He had once observed two Basques sitting across from each other in a train compartment. After a good long time sitting in silence, looking out the window, and occasionally lighting their pipes, one of them said, with a little puff of smoke, "I've bought myself a cow."

Long, eloquent silence. Then his neighbor responded, with emphasis: "I've got two cows on my place." Then definitive silence on the part of both. And my confrere added that, in all probability, when they got home, each one told his wife what a good, interesting, protracted conversation he'd had.

One may assume, and documentary evidence shows it, that Ignatius was not an artist with words, not a man to whom the gift of the word had been given in extraordinary measure. Actually, he was taciturn, reserved, often awkward in his formulations. This may be a first impression based on his ethnicity and its peculiar features. What biographical data, occurrences, or sidelights could be of interest as we seek to know something of his way, his manner of dealing with persons — his communication?

At Court: Schooled in Diplomacy

Ignatius was a man of the Basque aristocracy. The Loyolas were not of the high nobility, but were noble enough for us to apply to them a few clichés about the nobility. As far as prejudices are concerned, it is in any case interesting that these and not the contrary ones have arisen; and they can be fairly accurate, although they will be true of everyone in a different way and fit no one perfectly. "Aristocratic," in Ignatius's time, meant someone who "is somebody," who "has the say," and who cares somewhat about appearances, or at least who thinks that a person ought to care somewhat about appearances. One has a sense of style, or is chided when one offends against style. The nobility stick together and hold honor in high esteem. Loss of face and of honor are social death and are to be avoided like the plague.

An examination of Ignatius's formation shows that this is not just a general cliché, but that he had over ten years of formation at court, which marked him profoundly and which was determined by values and usages of a courtly kind. We must imagine what it means to have lived in a courtly milieu from the age of thirteen to twenty-six. There, the important questions include: What's in, what's out? Who's who? Who's where on the courtly career ladder? Who are this year's winners and losers? Who must be addressed and how? Who's having an affair, who's married, who's in league or in conflict with whom? Who is on whose side? How does one find the right diplomatic expression? Who can be a go-between between whom? Where is there intrigue, where are their coalitions, or who is likely to be betrayed? How are pacts made that will hold up? What's the latest court gossip? What do you have to know, whom do you have to know? And above all: Whom do I serve? To whom do I stand in a relationship of loyalty?

Ignatius was steeped in all of this. This was the atmosphere in which he lived from dawn to dusk. Surely he was trained in the use of weapons, surely he fought and he fenced, but he was never a soldier in the proper sense. He was a courtier. Almost more than of his fencing, he is proud of his calligraphy, as he himself stresses on one occasion. The first assignment he received was one not of a military leader, but of an administrative consultant for a city.

This approach is part of the recent scholarly trends in Ignatian studies: Ignatius and the way he handled communication must not be viewed mainly, or at least not exclusively, from the perspective of a military barracks. Ignatius was a person who had learned to move in the courtly world, the "worldly world."

He was usually very masterly and gallant, but not always: once, as folk barred his way in a narrow lane, he drew his sword, and only his companions kept him from initiating a small-scale blood-bath. He applied to the king for the right to bear arms and to have an armed valet, since an unknown person had long been threatening him with violence and death. One of Ignatius's biographers makes bold to suggest that there must have been a woman in the wings.

At Loyola: Looking Death in the Face

If his "milieu" — the outward, the courtly world, and his own hopes for his career — defined Ignatius's communication for decades, so his severe, life-threatening knee wound of 1521 occasioned a turning-point in his communication with God and a more profound communication with himself: with the powers, dynamics, and movements of his interior life.

The courtier, defender of the Castle of Pamplona, begins to notice such delicate motions within him as, for example, various gentle oscillations in his soul after the reading of a story of chivalry, or after meditation on Holy Scripture. Ignatius sees this as the start of the blossoming of a highly sensitive inner world — a world that strikes some of his critics as bordering on the pathological. While "the world," and some of his brothers, sail the world and seek to gain land, glory, and riches in America, Ignatius finds himself on an immense journey of discovery in the depths of his own soul. Now he plunges, or is plunged, into the world of sensations, feelings, fears, joys, emotions, movements, temptations, indecision, questions, uncertainties, drives, lures, stings of conscience, thoughts, movements of the will, decisions. And in them Ignatius begins to recognize the play of "laws." He begins to learn to swim in them, and to discover in them an entire cosmos: the cosmos of the soul, in which God's Spirit — as well as that of the Enemy — works without interruption.

He gets scant help from without. In vain does he seek — even "at considerable distance beyond the city" — repeatedly, spiritual experts and advisers, conversation partners. Apart from one old woman, who tells him she hopes Christ will meet him, he finds no one to give him the sense of being understood in his inmost depths. Ignatius always remained a lonely person, more on the reserved side, trusting but not familiar. "Alone and on Foot" is the appropriate title of a wonderful biography of Ignatius and is an expression used by Ignatius himself.

On the basis of experience of self, of intensive reflection on himself, and through having guided many persons, Ignatius learned the art of in-depth communication. Persons of every age, both sexes, and every social class opened to him the inmost parts of their soul and allowed him to touch the secret of their life. This might sound a bit technical, but an enormous field of research lay before Ignatius. He had gotten to know himself, and from that he learned the features of other people's lives that suited him.

On the Way: Alone and Together with Others

Not every stage in Ignatius's life can be matched with a reliable indication of place in order for us to be able to draw detailed conclusions about how his method of communication developed. He designated himself a pilgrim and was usually en route to somewhere: "alone and on foot." Perhaps it was this experience of solitude and loneliness, and being alone, that gave depth to his encounters. His encounters were not the result of an incapacity to be alone, which according to Blaise Pascal is the cause of all unhappiness.

Often alone, but often, too, with others, he was on the road, and it was especially then that he met so many persons: rich and poor, farmers and city-dwellers, persons of different religions, Inquisitors, merchants and sailors, bishops and simple faithful, young and old, those at death's door and those with a lust for life. In all of these encounters, his way of meeting others was tested, challenged, and subjected to a learning process. He was happy to have "spiritual conversations," met with countless individuals in personal, one-to-one conversations, heard confessions, consoled the sick and dying, preached in Italian despite his problems with the language; spoke gently to some and took others to court.

He could be wrathful, and, on other occasions, humorously playful, in a mixture of credulous naiveté and Ignatian shrewdness. Once when a gang of soldiers made a pass at two of the women in his company, he was "overcome with tremendous anger" and read them the riot act. His own judgment: "He did it so effectively, that the whole garrison of the house was paralyzed, and no one undertook the slightest action against him" (BDP, no. 38).

Once while walking a road between French and Spanish troops, he was suspected of espionage and taken prisoner: he had decided, despite fear of painful retribution, to address the captain not as "Your Grace," but as "you." This was how he dealt with everyone, as he "maintained the pious belief that Christ and the Apostles, and other saints, had spoken in this way.... Without showing the least formality or courtly politeness, he would answer crisply, with a noticeable pause after each word. The captain thought he was deranged and told those who had brought him to him, 'This one isn't quite right. Give him his stuff and throw him out of here' " (BDP, no. 53).

Some of Ignatius's later confreres seem to have had a similar gift in dealing with leaders and bosses. One of them, who had spent his whole life farming — and was now over ninety years old — got into a discussion during the Third Reich with a country mayor on the existence of God. Finally the rather slow and conceited "leader of men" thought he had the simple Jesuit brother with the argument, "God is invisible. I only believe in what I can see." The brother replied with a counter-question: "Have you ever seen your understanding, Mr. Mayor?" On a later occasion, having been sentenced by a judge either to go to jail immediately for several months or to pay five hundred marks "after the final victory," he settled for the latter penalty, and, when final victory was not the Führer's, got off scot-free.

Paris: Student, Spiritual Director, Friend of the "Friends in the Lord"

During Ignatius's student days in Paris, three influences and modes of expression stand out as shaping his approach to communication: his study, his role as a spiritual director, and his activity as friend of the Friends of Jesus.

It would take an entire chapter to set forth all of the possible determining influences in the years of study at the University of Paris on the ways of communication that grew in student and "Master Ignatius." Three concrete results can be easily and briefly indicated.

Study promoted *rational thinking*. While science, philosophy, and theology today in many areas operate under different assumptions and employ a different style of thought than they did in Ignatius's time, the fact remains that, at the renowned Sorbonne in Paris, one had to learn thinking, one had to compare the most divergent opinions. Ignatius studied this and sought to conform to it — hard enough at age thirty-six! There were things he may have learned especially in the frequent private and public disputations at which he must have assisted:

- First was *clarity of concepts*. What students usually experienced as dry learning was important for discussions: clarity when it came to concepts and definitions.

- Another element was of the greatest importance: practice in *listening*. Before introducing his own opinion, the disputant had to repeat what his adversary had said and obtain the latter's assent that his material had been repeated correctly. Then the first disputant might state his own view.

- Another important rule in the scholastic disputation was the *distinction*. One must make it clear in what sense one conceded an enunciation and in what sense not. In this way one always tried to find as much consensus as possible and to focus precisely on what was in dispute.

- Finally, still with our eye on the scholastic method: Ignatius had to learn to *assess the truth of the premises and validity of the argumentation on both sides.* Thomas Aquinas had made this his almost exclusive method. So it's not surprising that Ignatius, in his most significant document on communication, lays down the basic rule that one must always enunciate all arguments "pro and con" in order not to be seen as taking sides inappropriately or hastily.

Even in his most intimate assertions concerning "the seeking and finding of God in all things," Ignatius introduces the scholastic terminology found in Thomas Aquinas. God is present in all things through the divine "presence, power, and essence," writes Ignatius. The expression is Thomas's to the letter.

A second point became ever more clear during Ignatius's time in Paris: his role as *spiritual director* of persons who were on the way of encounter with God. This had begun in the preceding years, it is true, but in Paris it expanded. During this time, the Book of the Exercises, too, began to take shape: Ignatius's rich and varied experience in personal spiritual direction finds its reflection here. We might well single out two characteristics: first, Ignatius's emphasis on the individual as such, and the differences among individuals — a crucial trait of his spiritual direction. And second, his seeing himself not as a "director," but, pragmatically, as a simple companion — as the one who gives the Exercises, the directions for prayer — of the one "that receives them." It was the role of the exercitant and his openness to the operation of the Spirit of God in him that stood front and center, not "the director."

But more significantly still, at this time a close group of fellow students formed, from which the Society of Jesus grew. Doubtless Ignatius was the point of crystallization of the group, but for the young people it was just as clear that the common way of faith, life, and prayer brought them together. Ultimately, for them, it was Christ the Lord himself whom they primarily sought and found in the Exercises.

If the young community understood itself as "friends in the Lord," then this shows that Ignatius, too, was someone who felt himself bound to the others in this circle by a bond of friendship.

One of the first companions from this time, Simon Rodriguez, wrote, looking back on the time in Paris:

> Ignatius understood the art of dealing with persons and of binding them to himself through charming, winning behavior, to a degree which, to be honest, I have never found with anyone else.... He could gradually affect their hearts in such a way that, through his behavior, and through his pleasant, gentle speech, he carried all mightily away to the love of God. (BC, 240)

Here we see in a single sentence Ignatius's lovableness, his skill in communication, the crucial role he played, and the purposefulness of his encounters with persons — that is, the awakening of the love of God — brought to expression in one sentence. It is tragic that later confrontations brought Ignatius almost to the point of expelling this same Simon Rodriguez from the order. Doubtless it was only his respect for Simon's age and the echo of the old bonds of friendship that deterred Ignatius from this step. Masters of communication, too, must suffer difficulties and reach their limits. A similar case was that of another companion of the early years, Nicholas Bobadilla.

Just as tragic, perhaps, was the disappearance from his immediate environment of companions like Peter Faber, and especially Francis Xavier, with whom a genuine, deep personal friendship surely bound him, but who had received mission assignments. Yet perhaps this would also have been a help for his behavior, for his own development, for his dealings with persons, a gift that would have colored many of his character traits and manner. For all his bonding with his confreres, he alone had the task of the founding and leading of an enormously dynamic and rapidly growing order.

Rome: Founder and Leader of an Order

Ignatius never saw the order as "his" establishment in the proper sense. It was no empty platitude for him that the birth materialization of the new order was a gift of God and the work of the Holy Spirit. There is no manner of contradiction here with the fact that his very person and all of his abilities of communication and leadership were committed and involved. They were stamped and formed by this huge task. Much of what he had learned in his formation at court, as well as his strong goal orientation and other tendencies of his personality, here found their expression and shaping on an entirely different, unique level.

In what did Ignatius's most important traits consist? How did he "seem" to others in his manner of communication?

"He Seems All Love"

Since there were more people than just his housemate and admirer Father da Câmara, we may safely accept the general verdict on Ignatius: "He is always more inclined to love, in fact so much, that he seems all love. And so he is so universally loved by all, that one knows of no one in the Society who would not have a very great love for him, and would not judge that he is very much loved by the Father" (MEVI, no. 86). This was the judgment even of those who were closest to him — those with whom Ignatius was most strict, and to whom he said that his love was not correctly appraised if it were to be judged by his sometimes very harsh expressions.

Da Câmara explains that Ignatius's love showed itself primarily in three ways: first, in the great *friendliness* he showed to everyone. Where he could be, Ignatius was very obliging and courteous. When he noticed that he could make someone especially happy with fruit, he gave him fruit. Once, for the amusement of a confrere who lay ill, the slightly limping general danced — though he did ask the man not to call for an encore. And as he was very short, but wished to offer a gigantic

Fleming a loving consolation, he had to jump high to give the man a proper hug (MEVI, no. 47).

Second, he showed his love in the *"great concern* for the health of all, which is so great that it can scarcely be emphasized adequately" (MEVI, no. 88). Here Ignatius learned "the hard way": he had injured his health severely, for life, by his severe penitential exercises. But it was not only for the health of others that Ignatius had concern, but for all particulars and details about them. As he himself said, he would take an interest in his confreres' fleas. There was something downright motherly at work, when he unbuttoned his friend Francis Xavier's cassock, as he was bidding him farewell for his trip to Portugal and India, to make sure he had a warm shirt on.

Third, da Câmara added, Ignatius always took the gentle role; he never personally handled "matters that could be unpleasant for his subordinates." Not infrequently, the task fell to da Câmara. Ignatius once explained this division of labor to him with a comparison from the kitchen. A good salad, it seems, needs oil and vinegar. He, Ignatius, would supply the oil, and da Câmara the vinegar. Did da Câmara like this distribution of roles? Certainly not. A confrere once told him that he was "all vinegar." True, it is also reported that Ignatius could certainly "lambaste" his confreres — so effectively that there was an expression for it: someone would "get a hat" from him.

Loving Reverence

The question could arise: when did the tough, military, worldly communicator Ignatius step more clearly to the fore? The answer requires the patience that Ignatius himself could only learn, but that left its mark on him. Looking back on the early days of his conversion, he once observed that, although he wished to live entirely in the ways of God, he was nevertheless so blind that he had no sense of "humility, love, and patience."

More than two decades later, at the age of fifty-three, he felt himself drawn into an inward experience, lasting for days, which he felt as one of the altogether great graces of his life. He noticed that his inner world was taking on more and more the spiritual timbre and color of a "loving reverence." It was directed first of all to God, but then to everything else — persons, the cosmos, "all things." He acknowledged this as the way that God had personally chosen for him to follow.

Without attention to this, one would come to an altogether mistaken estimation of Ignatius's character and manner of communication. Without the tone, the reflection, the radiance of this loving reverence, all of his prudence and readiness in the ways of the world would lack warmth, reverence, sincerity, love. Then we should be without what for Paul, in the famous thirteenth chapter of his First Letter to the Corinthians, is the quintessence: without love, everything is — nothing. Without love, Ignatius's prudence would be cunning, his elegance sheer worldliness, his realism sheer pragmatism, his strategic thinking manipulation.

Realistic: "What's the Point?"

Formulations like "What's the point?" or "Get to the point" could have been coined by Ignatius. What interested him when it came to plans and decisions — the general of an order is almost always busy with decisions — was cutting to the chase, concrete relations and circumstances, persons, networks of relationship, probabilities, obstacles, helps. Nothing was more to his distaste than pointless chatter. But when he called on someone for an expert opinion, then he would readily listen to any number of viewpoints, helps for argumentation, and essential data. Of course, it had to be formulated briefly and appropriately.

Da Câmara once characterized Ignatius's manner of speech with the following words.

(1) That he never tries to convince with feelings, but with concrete things. (2) That he did not attempt to beautify matters with words, but allowed matters themselves to speak: he could cite so many circumstances, and cite them so ef-

fectively, that they carried an all but overwhelming weight
of conviction. (3) That his narrative style was simple, and
crystal-clear. And he had such a memory for things, and
even for words of importance, that he gave an account of an
occurrence ten, fifteen, or more times exactly as it occurred,
and he places it before his listener's eyes; and on important
matters he gives verbatim reports. (MEVI, no. 99)

Were we to seek to identify Ignatius from such characteristics
alone — there are many near-synonyms here — that is, were we
to see him as a merely factual person, as it were a sober, un-
emotional type, we should be very far from the mark. Affairs,
persons, activity, reality are elements of life for Ignatius. In the
last climax of the Exercises, in his Contemplation for Obtaining Love, he observes that love is exhibited more in deeds than
in words (GU, no. 230). This conceptualization is the prelude
to a matter-of-factness that gives direction to all else besides.
Ignatius's concern is for — inadequate as the formulation may
sound — "matters of love," real love. Real love, for him, is concrete, incarnated love, and occurs amid all real occurrences, "in
all things," as he says.

Sensible

There is no summing Ignatius up in a single word like "sensible," "smart," or "practical" to denote the manner of his
exchanges with others. A whole series of cognate concepts is
apposite here: expert, circumspect, experienced, wise, deliberate, organized, and so forth. Ignatius once said something to a
confrere that shows the extraordinary emphasis he placed on
practical exchanges with persons, places, and things:

> In and of themselves, innocence and holiness are of far
> more worth than all else. However, unless prudence and
> agility in dealing with others are likewise present, these
> persons are lacking something, and are incapable of lead-
> ing others. Eminent good sense, with a modicum of virtue,

is often of more worth for the leading of others than great holiness with paltry circumspection. At least, this holds in general. It is hard to make rules for the privileges God lends his saints. (BC, 299)

Even the last sentence is another piece of prudence: Ignatius will not absolutely contradict the possibility that there are saints of little circumspection who are nevertheless, through a grace of the Spirit, capable of leading. But he does not regard this as a normal case.

How did Ignatius's contemporaries regard his prudence? He listened and learned. After listening, he questioned. He observed his interlocutor exactly. With important persons, he acquainted himself in advance with the material to be discussed and with the person with whom he would be discussing it. He considered, slept on, a matter. He held conversations with experts. He had detailed opinions drawn up and protocols of important occurrences prepared. He had an excellent memory. He wrote many important letters with all care, and occasionally two or three times over. He took counsel of his advisers. He systematically weighed viewpoints and arguments for and against a position. He sought possible alternatives.

Ignatius did not have the profile of a hothead, a broker on the stock-market floor, who makes one decision after another just on "gut feeling" or "higher intuition." He approached things carefully, thinking them through in advance. And yet he was no mere cerebral type: he took time to bring decisions to prayer; he saw his thinking and planning as cooperation with God's prescience; he lived and thought out of deep trust in God. And he once said: being all too judicious is no sign of judiciousness. Judiciously said!

The Chief Quality: Reasonable — with a Flair

Judiciousness, with Ignatius, can also be denoted reasonableness. He himself was a reasonable person: "Since our Father was led in all things by reason, he was very much against doing things either from human inclination, or because profitable opportunities resulted" (MEVI, no. 288). Here we see that, for Ignatius, the decisive question was always: "What is good right now? What is reasonable and helpful to decide and do now?"

> It seems that in all matters Father lets himself be guided by reason.... And he holds this rule in all things, and prescribes it for others. And he says that this is what distinguishes human beings from the rest of animals. And this is the most, or one of the most, outstanding of our Father's qualities. (MEVI, no. 300)

It would be completely amiss to equate reasonableness with unfeeling, with a view to sheer effectiveness, with rationality. Ignatius worked on his environment not as a "brain," as we say, but as someone who obeyed reason. He would not have bought dishes on sale just because they were on sale, when the community had no need of them. He was wide awake when it came to any favorable opportunity; the crucial factor isn't "opportunity," however, but the weighing of what decision is sensible now.

It sounds paradoxical, but it is correct: much as Ignatius is famous for his "reasonableness," he relied just as much, in the context of the "discernment of spirits," on inner movements, sensibilities, and feelings. These he regarded as of the highest value. But here too, the fact remains: feelings serve as signposts, as warnings, as confirmation, but do not have the last word, which goes to the deeper sense and awareness of value oriented to Jesus Christ and the Spirit of God. Perhaps we could say: for the theory and practice of Ignatius's decisions, for his "supervisory meetings," argumentation and meditation, observation of the facts and profound prayer, an analysis of the situation and a cleansing of the world of feelings belong together. On occasion, he would insist with his governing team that they become more free of their evident fears, of their preferences and ambitions, since otherwise the meeting could not move ahead. Without freedom, there is no determination of what is better in a particular case. Decisions only with one's IQ, without the EQ, the emotion quotient, of which we have been hearing in recent years, are — seen from an Ignatian viewpoint — nonhuman, in the sense that the entire human being does not participate in the decision-making process.

At times, Ignatius's reason and feeling were put to the test. One day a man came to Rome who, on the grounds of an "inner inspiration," was solidly convinced that he was the pope and that all that was lacking was the official coronation. No one could shake his conviction. Finally he was sent to Ignatius. Ignatius told him simply that the church had only one pope. He must simply go to the Vatican and see whether the pope was still alive. If he was, the man should assume that his inspiration was wrong. There are no reports that Ignatius's efforts failed. It is not reported that Ignatius's intervention went wrong. We might say: a typically Ignatian kind of therapy. Perhaps we should call it "reality therapy."

Listening and Readiness to Learn

When someone is prudent, experienced, and competent, then it not infrequently happens that this expresses itself in an outward way, in his or her being a master at conversation. Such a person introduces ideas, poses alternatives, weighs advantages and disadvantages, sketches organizational schemata, states the conditions of his or her goals, and so on. The others can only listen in astonishment, or with a certain helplessness and unsureness wonder what their role is in the whole. This is not the profile of Ignatius Loyola's leadership personality. He was a great listener, a sensitive, patient listener in a spiritual conversation, in counseling individuals, in the Exercises. But he was also a listener when it came to the decision-making process. Therefore he gives as the first rule for his confreres at the Council of Trent to listen and learn, and to be thoughtful, careful, and slow in speech and judgments.

This listening is, in the best sense, "active listening" and holistic listening. Ignatius expressly emphasizes that one must attend to the content, feelings, and purposes of the person speaking. His attentiveness and, of course, his growing experience, as well, made it possible for him, as various testimonials report, in a short time to quickly and precisely figure out any interlocutor or situation and to react appropriately. His answers and conclusions were usually short, but clear and to the point. The listener could rightly have the impression of being personally understood and accepted, along with the words spoken on the occasion.

Single-minded and Persistent

There are personalities who are very prudent and very observant, who are the best possible supplier of ideas, but are unable consistently to translate their suggestions into reality. Ignatius not only had prudent ideas, great plans, but he also worked with all his strength to implement them. A number of things can be made out with regard to this ability to see things through.

First: Ignatius's *purposefulness*. "Purposefulness" is an essential category for him, and this concept occurs often in his vocabulary. "Whatever most helps for this purpose..." is a characteristic expression with him.

In immediate connection with his purposefulness is his *awareness of the means* and the relation of means to end, purpose and path. Whoever wills an end must also will the means to that end. In other words, the earnestness of the will with regard to the end is to be measured by the earnestness of the will to the means. To end a meeting with a simple decision for something, without a precise determination of the means, the "operationality," was unimaginable for Ignatius. Here we could invoke a military comparison: a decision for the defense of a city, or for a campaign, without a precise investigation of the military means and possibilities for mounting it, is unimaginable, or at least very dangerous.

Even when end and means are clear, the story is not over yet. Courage and, especially, *persistence* are necessary in order not to "throw in the towel" at the first sign of an obstacle. Obstacles, for Ignatius, were often a sign of the correctness of his undertaking. When something went on too long without an obstacle, he grew a bit uneasy. His conviction was that a great thing awakens contradiction. And so he is quoted as saying: "Whoever fears human beings will never accomplish anything great for God: nothing worthy of God can be done without setting the world on its ear" (BC, 238). A case in point is that Ignatius once waited fourteen hours at a cardinal's door until he could finally speak to him. Another cardinal, who played the part of protector and guardian angel for the order, coined the expression, with regard to Ignatius: "He has already driven the nail!" This coinage seems to have so "hit the nail on the head" that it became a common expression in Rome.

Ignatius had this kind of persistence, in the service of a goal once seen as correct, even with respect to church authorities. The first of such cases was when he would have renounced the founding of his order had he been required to prescribe the recitation of the Divine Office in choir, as at first it seemed he would be. But this was not the form of the order that Ignatius had conceived in the Spirit of God. When it seemed that one of his confreres, Francis Borgia, would be created a cardinal, he wrote that he would fight this with all of the means at his disposal, if he need be in the presence of the pope and the emperor, even if both saw things differently. True, Ignatius was realistic enough to say that it was useless to hold on to a matter out of pure stubbornness where there was no hope for its realization. This he regarded as a waste of energy and time (see BC, p. 238).

As with all of his character traits, his persistence too has to be distinguished from pig-headedness, which becomes clear once we understand the motivation for his persistence. The basic motivation for Ignatius was to seek and realize the will of God. Hundreds of his letters end with a formula such as: "May Christ our Lord give all of us the grace ever to sense his holy will, and to fulfill it completely" (BU, 875). Ignatius's entire existence, all of his striving, is dictated by this longing to let God's will be great and effective in his life. With this petition he begins every prayer session in his "general preparatory prayer." And in his manners of proceeding, his activities, his decisions, he orientates himself to the manner of Jesus, whom he once calls our "gentle Lord."

A confrere destined for work on Corsica wrote: "Daily, our Father returns to the notion that we should proceed with determination, as our Lord Jesus Christ has done; for with courage and humility, he says, everything can be done" (BC, 240).

Obviously Ignatius's basic will to help persons to their final goal, to their eternal happiness, had an effect on his dealings with them. He never proceeded blindly, but sought to orientate himself to what could help a person along the way of life, along the way of faith. It was a bad argument for him, then, when someone sought to enter the order only to get ahead. Without the decided will to help one's neighbor, Ignatius would allow no one into his apostolic society, and no true understanding of Ignatius's goal-directedness is possible.

Loyola Again: About Halfway Up

In 1986 I spent some days at Loyola, Ignatius's birthplace. On a free day, I made a tour of one of the heights nearby. Halfway up, I left the group and headed for the peak. After some time I came to a grove of trees such as I had never seen in my life. They must have been beeches. They were strangely small, but otherwise fully grown trees. They were all proper beech trees, but their trunks were only five or six feet tall, and their tops only twice as tall as that. They were like overgrown Japanese Bonsai trees, or even like young, but full-grown, beeches. They reminded me — it may sound strange — of Ignatius: a full-grown figure, but not overly large, powerful and uncommonly compact, but not exaggeratedly muscular. And this tree was in a group of trees, but not dwarfed by a wood; drawing all of its strength from very harsh soil, but not to the point of exhausting it; on the upper part of the height, but not out of sight of the valley.

To put it in less flowery, or less arboreal, fashion: the radiance of Ignatius could be described with words like: observant, listening, sensitive, feeling, goal-oriented, decisive, consistent, reasoned, reverent, attached to God, loving.

Where a person's strengths lie, there the corresponding threats are most at home. Those working most closely with Ignatius might have wished he could devote more time and attention to them; his harshness made many a man groan. Many a dismissal from the order was sudden, and with one night's warning. His bent for perfection even drove the aging Ignatius to publish rules for free days, which became known as "vineyard rules."

What strikes one in his personality is the dynamic combination of polarities and tensions. If you know only a few stories, you can come to a crass error in judgment. Ignatius was at once rationally oriented and capable of shedding tears every day. He strove with all of his might, and yet completely trusted in God. He worked very hard himself, wherever he could, and yet delegated everything possible, with a carte-blanche. He was modest, and yet publicized everything conducive to a "good press" for the order. He had clear ideals, and yet he reacted to all persons and situations with elasticity. He was self-controlled, and yet would suddenly flash forth with waggery, humor, and something like irony. He was so sensitive, due to his severely injured health, that it sometimes caused him distress to put on his cold shirt in the morning, and yet he appeared constantly serene. He was an expert in communication, and yet worked with reserve. He was attached to God — amid everyday events.

Much must be said of his highly complex personality in order to grasp it even a little, and yet the declaration of a certain person who was considered possessed says a great deal: "Oh, the little Spaniard, who limps and has such merry eyes!"

Chapter 2

The Key Text

"Instructions for Communication"

We speak of a "key event" when we are suddenly favored with an approach to a person, an area of life, or indeed to a literary text through an occurrence, an encounter, a happening. A certain poem can have been someone's key to Goethe, another may have discovered a fascination with jazz through a trumpet piece by Louis Armstrong. My key event, the occurrence that unlocked for me, many years ago, communication as a decisive perspective of Ignatian spirituality, was the reading of a longish piece of Ignatius's bearing the title, "Instruction for the Conference in Trent." By the "Conference in Trent," he meant the famous Council of Trent. The instruction, composed in the beginning of the year 1546, is addressed to Jesuits Jay, Laínez, and Salmerón, who were to take part in the Council as theological *periti*. This piece will now be presented, in particular the part in it that deals with communication.

The Key Text

The document itself and its general introduction are remarkable. Instructions weren't automatically drawn up for such an occasion. This alone is testimony to Ignatius's consciousness of style. It is no wonder, then, that the first Jesuits spoke again and again of "our manner of proceeding" (*noster modus procedendi*). Meetings often go off on tangents because their whole course, as well as the interventions and style of speech of the participants, is prepared in too much of a dilettante style, or not with the right "feel" on the part of the participants. Like the instruction as a whole, the major subheadings are themselves remarkable.

The first part is written "For dealing with others," for communication with the participants in the Council. It will form the principal part, and the following explanations will be built on it. But let us notice beforehand: even before Ignatius had written a single explicit word about communication, he had already made a basic decision: he saw the Council not as an occurrence concerned with a defense or deeper understanding of old truths or with rejecting heresies; the Council for Ignatius is in good part an extraordinary and intensive communication event. Therefore he recommends to his confreres not that they take with them the latest theological lexicon, but that they pay attention to their manner of communication. Precisely because the Council is ultimately concerned with *communio*, with mutual community — or, perhaps, with excommunication — an attentive, loving behavior with one another is just as important as the clarification of concepts or theological declarations.

The second part is headed "In Order to Assist Souls" and deals with the pastoral activity of the Jesuits during the Council. The power and influence residing therein can be shown by a single quotation: "To visit the sick in hospitals at an hour or hours of the day that will be most helpful for their bodily health; hear the confessions of the poor, and console them, and even, when it is possible, bring them something" (BU, 114).

One could ask here: What would it mean if, at councils and synods today, the participants catechized children "on the side," visited the sick, and brought gifts to the poor? Would this not lend theological decisions more credibility and effectiveness and provide greater interpretative support?

The last part, with the heading "In Order the More to Help One Another," deals with common decisions and the daily report on how each observed the others in the events of conciliar communication.

Introduction: The Cross and the Name

Ignatius often sketched a little cross on his letters, and this is the case with the instruction for Trent. This little cross is Ignatius's "logo," his trademark. It expresses a fundamental spiritual experience of his faith and his life. It's a question of enduring and withstanding the cross — or to put it in more everyday terms, tensions, confrontations, pains, struggle, confusion, opposition. Where are tensions and the cross more to be experienced than when communication among persons misses the mark, beginning with everyday annoying misunderstandings, wounding remarks, and, at the other extreme, hate-filled "deathly silence"?

The cross has a name: the name of Jesus. Ignatius writes it on the page. This may well proclaim that what follows is not only a matter of communication, of not breaking rules, of skills and cleverness, of manipulative verbal games, but of successful or utterly failed encounters. In either kind of human communication we also see a reflection of the relationship between God and human beings, as in the unity of love of God and neighbor.

The little cross, in connection with the name of Jesus, can perhaps remind one of Jesus' communication on his way of the cross: Of his taking his distance from Peter, who is unwilling to accompany him on this way: "Get behind me, Satan!" Of his question to the man who struck him, "Why do you strike me; have I done you an injustice?" Of his silence before Pilate and the vociferous, inflamed crowd. Of his reconciling word regarding his mockers and executioners, "Father, forgive them, they know not what they do!" Of his trustful question, the last cry of his life and at the same time his death cry, "My God, my God, why have you forsaken me?" Was Ignatius thinking these things as he sketched the little cross on his letter? Perhaps no, perhaps yes. At all events, he likewise drew, on a piece of writing containing several observations, a little cross, and wrote under it, "Jesus, my love, is crucified." Perhaps this expression says two things: that Jesus, whom he loves, is crucified; but also that his own loving feels the burden of the cross.

The First Rule: Learning to See
the Surpassing Worth of Conversation

Just as much is gained, by God's grace, from dealing with
many persons for the salvation and spiritual progress of
souls; conversely, in such dealings much is lost on our side
and sometimes on both sides, if we are not alert and blessed
with the Lord's favor.

And as our calling makes it impossible to avoid such
commerce, we shall walk the more peacefully in our Lord,
the more we seek to see things in advance, and direct
ourselves with some order.

There follow certain things from which, or from other
things like them, we may have utility in our Lord: one may
omit them or apply them. (BU, 112)

The first major statement of this instruction means that conversation is valuable, that much can be won or much lost. This
view appears to be anything but self-evident! For some people,
the old saying of the philosopher Seneca, "I've found that every
time when I go out, I come back a worse human being," probably doesn't sound all that unpleasant and unreal. Even Ignatius's
text cites the "impossibility of avoiding such commerce" — to
be sure, in a context of the calling and profile of his community,
which involves constant contact with persons. Here, naturally,
personal, pastoral conversation, commerce with one another, has
a high value.

It seems to me worthy of mention in this text, as well, that
Ignatius by no means assigns the guilt for a failed conversation
to himself alone. The cause may lie with the one, the other, or
both sides. This is likewise the only viewpoint that allows us to
clearly recognize mistakes in communication and then, perhaps,
to avoid them.

Along with care and concern to avoid mistakes, however,
stands the insight of faith that a really successful conversation
is a gift. Neither the best conversational technique nor the most

careful preparation guarantees that a conversation will go well. Thus, a conversation is the responsibility of everyone who takes part in it. The decisive preparation and cooperation consists in being *watchful and attentive*. The truth of this statement is shown in the very fact that nothing destroys a conversation so quickly and completely as the impression that one's partner is simply paying no attention. There are, it is true, conversationalists who seem to be sleeping, but are, oddly, awake and present just at the decisive moment. Still, signs of weariness are not exactly encouraging to the others. The story is told of a Jesuit who was chairing a conference and who rose from his place, thanked the group, and only then realized from everyone's laughter that he had simply woken up during a brief pause by the speaker.

For Ignatius, vigilance is, so to speak, a virtue of the Jesuit calling, since it belongs to the Jesuit task to be among persons. As in the Exercises the little preludes are important for the meditation, so with a conversation preparation is important. To be foresighted enough to "dispose" oneself, to be in the "right frame of mind" for a conversation, includes taking oneself, the others, and the encounter, seriously.

In conclusion, Ignatius observes that many different instructions are helpful for conversations, but that one need not have them all in one's head: one may "omit them or apply them." With the flood of materials on communication available in our day, it is worth noting that while we may leave out many things, we do have to pay attention to some essential rules of the game.

The Second Rule: Slow of Speech, Carefully, and Affectionately

Second: I would be slow of speech, careful, and affectionate, especially when expounding things that will be dealt with, or could be dealt with, in the Council. (BU, 112)

This is not the only time that Ignatius enjoins slow speech. Perhaps this comment was especially important with his southern confreres. But the "discovery of slow speech" seems more and more important for us northerners as well. On my return from a ten-year stay in Rome, I had the impression that in Germany, too, the tempo of speech both on television and in everyday conversation had accelerated. One of the most frequent expressions of the moderators on television and radio is the formulation "Can you add something very briefly. In one sentence, please."

It sometimes strikes one as downright grotesque when a person on a program is asked to sum up the most difficult issues in a single sentence, concretely and "very simply" — without "oversimplification," of course. The poverty-stricken condition of Europeans who "have no time" — in contrast to many people in poor countries — often makes it impossible to have a quiet conversation. I remember how, on occasional visits to East Germany before reunification, I had the repeated impression that persons there had more time and leisure for conversations. Under pressure of time, a good conversation can be held only with difficulty. It is fun, of course, to bat words back and forth like tennis balls, on occasion. Brilliant conversational Ping-Pong, with its smashes and slices, *can* sometimes be enjoyable. But what we need most of all is this, that we repeatedly pass the word to one another again and again like a piece of bread that can be passed, chewed, tasted, and digested in peace. Only in this way will words be nourishing. And this is what Jesus meant when he said: "One does not live by bread alone, but by every word that comes from the mouth of God" (Matt. 4:4).

A virtue closely related to slowness is called *care*. Sometimes someone speaks so rapidly as to give the impression of speaking more rapidly than thinking. The motto of these persons seems to be, "How shall I know what I think unless I first hear what I say?" Such rapid-fire speech sometimes makes us completely lose sight of the persons who are expressing and revealing themselves in it. The idiom "There is talk" can sometimes be more to the point than calling it "communication."

The invitation to speak not just deliberately but also thoughtfully, also means not rushing into decisions. Always allow

yourself the self-critical question: Have I made myself sufficiently clear? Do I understand the standpoints of the others with
sufficient precision?

Specifically with disputed theological and pastoral themes, it is
crucial to speak thoughtfully, carefully, and also *affectionately*.
This directive will be not only for the times of the Council of
Trent, but also for the times after Vatican II. How many hasty
reactions, rigid positions, unloving judgments and ineffective
"muzzling," from above as from below, hamper conversations
and fruitful pastoral ministry?

The Third Rule: Listening, and Peaceful Attention to the Whole Person

The third rule could be dubbed, Ignatius's "golden rule of
communication":

> Third: I would be slow of speech, that I may listen to ad-
> vantage; calm, in order to feel and become acquainted with
> the positions, feelings, and wills of those who speak — in
> order to respond better or to keep silent. (BU, 112)

On this sentence there is almost nothing to be said but that it
is in a certain way a feast for the palate. What Ignatius says in his
Book of the Exercises is applicable here: one should "savor" the
words (GU, no. 2). Almost every word could supply a chapter
heading of its own.

The repeated advice, "I would be slow in speaking," could
itself be seen as a more gentle form of instruction, because it
takes on the form of a personal witness and does not speak in
the imperative, as in "Slow down!" No, instead it goes: "I would
be slow in speaking." Speaking slowly helps one to listen better. That's what it's all about, using your ears, "to try to learn
through hearing," as another translation has it. It is not a matter
of listening in on someone, or spying on someone. Affectionate
listening opens to another the space in which that other can exist.
The good listener authorizes the speaker to speak. Such listening

can only be that of someone who does not live with the notion that he or she knows everything anyway, knows it better than the others do, and actually doesn't need to listen anymore. To speak before and with notorious know-it-alls is a torment, or just impossible. It can all but "drive one up the wall," although Ignatius recommends an effort to *remain calm*.

In almost every handbook of communication, there is a section pointing out that during conversation part of our attention should keep coming back to our feelings. When one notices that one's inner peace diminishes or is lost, then there is danger. A simple analogy can make this clear. Sometimes landscapes, things, persons, are mirrored in a peaceful lake or pond so clearly that in a photograph it is difficult to distinguish what is image and what is reflected image. Analogously, one ought to see whether the "waters of the soul" are peaceful enough that one can form a clear image within oneself of what the other is saying. When one's own interior is like water churned and whipped up by anger, inhibition, fear, rebellion, and so on, then everything in the reflection is distorted. That's just how it happens in the New Testament story of the disciples' terror in the storm on the Sea of Galilee: Instead of Jesus, they think they see a ghost. Many encounters take on such a ghostly character. In that case, one should call "time out," take a "break," and seek to become inwardly calm.

Inward calm will likely help one to encounter one's conversation partner attentively and to take account of the various levels, the various dimensions of the person. Ignatius cites thoughts, feelings, and wills. This says three things for good listening.

On a first level, it is a matter of attending to the *content of the enunciation*, the message, the matter, the objective. Here the decisive question is: *What* is the other saying? Could I repeat the words correctly?

The second level to which attention should be paid consists of *feelings*. The contents of the message are far from exhausting what it says, and far from constituting communication. Human beings have feelings too. These are essential. Only when I know why someone, for example, battles so sturdily for something, that is, why he or she has such fear of something or so earnestly seeks to defend a value, only then do I know what my correspondent is concerned with. Only then may I perhaps dispel unfounded fears by seeking to show that a value that the other sees as threatened will by no means be destroyed. With a conversational impasse, often the most helpful questions to put to oneself or to my conversation partner are such as: "What am I so afraid of, and why? How did I come to this experience of value?" If this can be expressed, it is often possible to get the conversation moving again.

The third level is that of *willing*, the actual intentions. Knowledge of this level takes into account the realization that, behind a statement whose content is very simple, deeper intentions can lie. Often statements are really only trial balloons to test reactions, and only then does the famous "real" or "true intent" come out. Hence it is sensible to bracket a first declaration cautiously and see whether there is not something else involved. Sometimes a person does not precisely know what she or he wishes. Then it is the time to perform the work of a midwife so that the real longing, the real wish, the real intention may be voiced.

It is significant how Ignatius characterizes the perception of thoughts, feeling, and willing, and what is supposed to happen with them. In the process he considers the three levels just mentioned. Listeners, too, should listen as complete persons. They should *sense* what corresponds to the feeling, *reflect*, and *decide* whether it is better to speak or to remain silent.

The first question, then, is: Do I *feel* anything from the other? Is there a resonance in myself as I listen? This is practically the same thing as what is nowadays called "empathy," capacity for feeling the feelings of another. In the absence of a certain capacity for sharing one's feelings, no helpful relationship is possible on the personal level.

The second question is: Do I see, do I *recognize*, what the other says? Do I really perceive the content of the message, or am I merely bewildered? One merely caught in the maelstrom of another's feelings no longer has the capacity for genuine understanding. The latter may require a conceptual effort, the "straining to grasp the concept" (Hegel). Recognition means getting acquainted. Often enough, I must first ask: What are the facts and arguments that someone is putting forth? What are the experiences that he or she has had and that underlie those arguments?

The third and last question relates to the *decision*. Shall I answer or be silent? We might miss, or we might be struck by, the fact that Ignatius closes the sentence not with "...whether it is better to answer," but with "...whether it is better to keep silent." Normally, quite a few persons taking part in a conversation are pressured to give answers. In this case there must be a conscious decision: Does it seem to me better to answer, or more in keeping with the purpose to remain silent? Well-qualified answer or well-qualified silence, that is the question.

The Fourth Rule: Freedom from Prejudice

Scarcely anything comes in for such critical scrutiny as do prejudices: prejudices against foreigners, against atheists, against intellectuals, against gays, against Christians (the last are sometimes seen as not so bad), and so forth. Being unprejudiced often scores as a high democratic virtue. Of course Ignatius did not use all of our jargon, but what he says about balanced, free, and authentic dealing with the matter at hand — and this often includes interaction, as well — is worthy of consideration:

> When the conversation is on the same matter or others, [one should] give reasons for both sides, lest one show oneself impaired by one's own judgment. I should make an effort to leave no one unsatisfied. (BU, 112)

I remember how a few years ago I made a motion in a small prayer group and explained why a small change in the liturgy seemed to me a meaningful one to make. By way of conclusion, I also presented viewpoints that contained certain misgivings about my own proposal. The astonishment was considerable. Surely when persons want to get a proposal through, they cannot at the same time cite grounds against it!

Ignatius could. He even found it decidedly helpful. First, in concrete decision-making it seldom or never happens that one position has everything going for it while the others are pure nonsense. Second, such a consideration brings it to expression that the one making the suggestion has really "thought it over," even considering opposing arguments. Third, this signals any potential "adversary" that we credit him or her with thinking ability and good reasons. In turn, this can help such "adversaries" more easily to take new thoughts in earnest. Not least of all, by arguing in a way open to all sides, we demonstrate that we are not primarily intent on having our own cause or ourselves prevail at all costs, but that our primary interest is to determine what is presumably best for the "cause," for example, for a community and so on. In plain religious language: it is a matter of seeking the will of God and not simply a matter of pushing through one's own interest.

This non-partisan, nuanced approach helps produce an atmosphere of understanding and respect. It contributes to "leaving no one dissatisfied." It could make a great deal of difference what we rejoice over at the close of a conversation or discussion: Are we glad that we "gave it to the others but good," that we were able to devastate the arguments of the other side piece by piece and make them the butt of laughter? Or are we satisfied when we have the impression that the others, too, are happy with the course of the conversation and that we have contributed something to this?

On his hundredth birthday, Jesuit Oswald von Nell-Breuning, who died in 1991 at the age of 101, gave a talk to express his gratitude for all that he had received. In it he set forth the secret of the high regard in which he was held in society, church, and state, as well as in the area of his scholarly achievements. In this testimonial he set an example precisely of these rules for freedom from prejudice. He said:

[The thought has occurred to me] to inform you of the method I apply and should like to recommend to and enjoin on everyone who will come after me. I refer to the procedure of recognizing, completely and wholly, right to the dot over an *i,* the part of truth obtaining in the opinion of an adversary. For me, this is first of all a rule of intellectual honesty. But in addition, I hold it for the most suitable and promising procedure methodologically as well. From what do most false teachings get their attraction? They get it from the amount of truth they contain. And if I prove to my adversary in a discussion that I know of these elements of truth, that I share them with him, then he knows, first of all, that I have understood him, and that I have the wish to understand him aright. And thereby I win his sympathy to begin with — his readiness to try to understand me aright as well, so that we may join dialogue with each other over the matter at issue, and not merely thresh straw in a pseudo-conversation in which each understands something different by the *termini*, the terms, being used. Here I refer to the kind of "conversation" in which one believes that one agrees with one's conversation partner, whereas in reality the two are miles apart. Or just the other way about, one believes that one is caught up in a battle, whereas in reality each partner means the same thing. I think I may boast of having practiced this manner of procedure with utter consistency. And I think I shall not be accused of arrogance if I say that this is the explanation for a great part of the respect I enjoy even in circles far removed from the church and religious faith.

The Fifth Rule: Caution with Regard to Arguments from Authority

Sometimes one can defend oneself in conversations by giving one's partner to understand that he or she has now used a "killer sentence." This is not a reproach that one would ordinarily welcome. Killer sentences are turns of phrase that deal a fatal blow to a conversation. "No one would be so stupid as to.... What you say is really out of date.... Nobody in the world but you holds.... The experts all say the opposite is true.... That was never the case.... So long as I have anything to say around here...." *Roma locuta, causa finita:* "Rome has spoken, the case is closed!"

When words like these occur in a conversation, then the question rightly arises whether it is still a matter of a vital back-and-forth, or whether a real conversation is being carried straight to the grave. What does Ignatius think of the matter?

"I would not call in any persons as authorities, especially not when they are great persons, except in things already extensively considered. I must be on good terms with everyone and have a passion for no one" (BU, 113).

That sort of statement might surprise people who think Ignatius was just a true-believing medieval Christian. But it is true: despite all of the loyalty of Ignatius Loyola, despite all of his obvious respect for authority, Ignatius knows too that there are situations in which an appeal to authorities and names rather harms the quest for truth than serves it. It is normally not helpful for a conversation when the various sides only cite their respective authorities: "Ratzinger says.... But Drewermann writes.... Küng has said...." Surely a person in a conversation ought to be able to cite other persons, but only meaningfully, in order to present interesting viewpoints, important considerations and arguments, and not in order to stop the mouths of others through the mere naming of authorities. The decisive self-critical question is: Am I free, or am I "passionate" in the sense of an inner constraint, a prejudice, a wrongly understood esprit de corps, a personal idée fixe?

In these questions, it is clear once more that an approach to truth is a matter not only of material, objective, rational considerations, but at the same time of inner freedom. Where someone is inhibited by fears and fixations, it will be difficult for that person to rethink anything, to "be converted" or do an about-face in respect of the matter at issue, to stay on the track of truth or to seek it. One will scarcely feel Paul's inner impetus to wish to be "all things to all people." It certainly is not easy to be on good terms with everyone. "Try to please everyone," the popular saying has it, "and you'll please no one." And it is also certain that the one who will please the most persons possible, indeed everyone, has his work cut out for him. Often enough he falls not between two stools, but between all of them. Of course, this may often be the best place for a Christian to sit — better, at all events, than to make oneself comfortable everywhere.

The Sixth Rule: Modest Lucidity

Altogether along the same line lies the sixth point of the instruction for the Council of Trent:

> When the things spoken of are so true that one cannot or ought not to keep silence, one should state one's position with the greatest possible calm and humility, and close with *salvo meliore judicio* — "unless there is a better opinion." (BU, 113)

This affirmation establishes that one should not constantly hesitate to speak, out of fear of giving offense to another by coming out and taking a position. Conversely, one ought not to express oneself out of a simple wish to be noticed and to impress hearers through one's pretended certainty. It is helpful for a fruitful dialogue when, in the style of one's speech and even, perhaps, in expressive turns of rhetoric, it becomes recognizable that one does not take oneself for infallible. Are there not more than a few of us who, while refusing to ascribe to the pope any kind of infallibility, are nevertheless highly incensed when our own statements are critically scrutinized? In the interest of the hygiene of the soul, it may be worthwhile often to enter into conversation with "the pope in us," "the pope in me." Surely an interesting dialogue will occasionally come of it.

The Seventh Rule: Taking Enough Time

A short text of Paul Konrad Kurz can serve as the pitiless mirror in which we can perhaps see much of ourselves: "Time. Momo [a children's fictional character] has time. A Turk has time. God has time. The pastor has no time. A regular German." Ignatius also speaks of having time in his rules:

> In general: In speaking together about, and dealing with, acquired or infused matters, it is a very great help, when I wish to speak about them, not to attend to my free time or lack of it, or let it be seen that I am in haste — that is, not to whether it is convenient for me, but whether it is convenient and suitable for the person with whom I seek to deal, in order to move that person to the greater glory of God. (BU, 113)

Granted, nowadays it is a matter of the spiritual health of not a few persons who do pastoral work that they must, after all, learn to say no and to see that their appointment calendar isn't bursting at the seams. Certainly we should attend to ourselves as well, and not only to others. But it is just as true that we need time when difficult matters are up for discussion.

If we go to someone with a personal issue, something that affects our life and inner self, and we notice that the intended adviser "really does not have time," we will not so readily seek conversation. Here it is better to postpone the conversation or to recommend another conversation partner than repeatedly to neglect scheduled appointments, to shorten the conversation, or to let it be interrupted by telephone calls. Time is one of the most precious gifts that we can give to one another. But here too, "God loveth a cheerful giver." And just so, God surely loves those who can accept their own boundaries and say a friendly, regretful "No."

How one deals with time is a way of showing reverence for God and human beings and of "being in the state of grace." At any rate, author Peter Handke once suggested translating this old catechism expression as being "in the state of having time."

Practice

Ignatius would not be Ignatius if he merely produced beautiful words and helpful rules and left it at that. He knows that everything demands practice. Therefore he ends his instructions with a passage dealing with daily practice. First, each individual should attend to what is important to him. Second, however, the three Jesuit confreres are to sit together for an hour each evening, look back on the day, review their decisions, and plan the course of their future activity. Just so, they should likewise call one another's attention to what they have noticed in one another's manner of communication.

Having carefully formulated his instructions, Ignatius ends them decisively: "This ordinance begins within five days after our arrival in Trent. Amen."

Chapter 3

Basic Attitudes

Nourishment of Communication

Psychologist and widely read author Paul Watzlawick wrote in his *Anleitung zum Unglücklichsein* (Instructions for being unhappy) a deliciously macabre story:

> A man wants to hang a picture. He has the nail, but no hammer. His neighbor has one. And so our man decides to go next door and borrow it. But he hesitates: "What if my neighbor won't lend me the hammer? Yesterday he greeted me so hastily. Perhaps he was in a hurry. But perhaps the hurry was only an excuse; maybe he has something against me? Well, what? I haven't done anything to him; it's just his imagination. If someone wanted to borrow a tool from me, *I* would give it to him right away. Then why won't he? How can a person deny so simple a favor to his neighbor? People like this jerk are the ruination of others. And he also imagines I'm dependent on him for his hammer. Just because he has a hammer. I've had it up to here." And so he storms to his neighbor's house and rings the bell. The neighbor opens the door, but before he can say his friendly "Good morning" our man shouts at him, "You can just keep your hammer, you idiot!" (Watzlawick, 35)

The story makes us laugh presumably because, on the one hand, it makes a very clear point by exaggerating; while, on the other hand, we feel: Is it really only a gross exaggeration? Aren't our lives often mentally engaged in quite similar fantasy-conversations, and isn't our behavior often prompted by attitudes and feelings of mistrust, ego, annoyance, and so on?

The angry word, the shut or even open door, are only the outward, visible signs of communication. All behaviors are based on attitudes. Words are the fruit of inner stirrings, as Jesus once observed apropos of cleaning vessels: "Evil and good come from the heart." A person in quest of communication, or of an improvement in communication, must not only look for polite turns of phrase in a book of etiquette, but must be concerned with views, attitudes, and the cultivation of the world of feelings. Ignatius has very extensive material here, and we can learn a great deal from it.

"So Blind…":
Humility, Love, and Patience

One of the best known and most grotesque of the stories in Ignatius's autobiographical report is the account of a faith dialogue gone far and painfully astray. It shows how the behavior of a person feeds on feelings, opinions, ideals, and impressions. In the case at hand, this mixture was so explosive in Ignatius that it just missed making him a murderer.

Already in the process of his conversion, Ignatius was riding side by side with a Moor. The two got into a conversation. The question of Mary's virginity came up. "The Moor stated that he could well believe that the Virgin conceived without having known a man. But that she remained a virgin after Jesus' birth, that he could not believe" (BDP, no. 15). Despite all theological arguments, Ignatius failed to convince the Moor of his opinion. Apparently Ignatius was growing angry; in any case, the Moor now rode on ahead.

Ignatius describes the condition of his soul by telling us that he fell into "an inner turmoil" that left his soul very dissatisfied. For he believed he had not sufficiently done his duty" (ibid.) He was overwhelmed with the desire to ride after the Moor and — to avenge Mary's honor — stab him to death. Not that he was completely sure he ought to do this, so he finally left it to his mule to make the decision: if it followed the Moor, who had ridden into a village, out comes the dagger; if it took the other fork and rode past the village, then he would leave his conversation partner alone. To his great astonishment, the mule did not go in the direction of the village, although every fairly reasonable mule heads for where there is something to drink and where it can get a rest.

Ignatius recounts this story not for the amusement of his audience, but because he believes that this experience may be worth telling "in order the better to understand how our Lord proceeded with this soul, which was still altogether blind despite its great desire to serve him in every way, as well as it could understand" (BDP, no. 14).

What does Ignatius wish to say with this piece of spiritual pedagogy in the form of a story? He wants to tell his readers and confreres that someone can be "so advanced" that he wishes to live solely to please God, in other words that someone can stop being motivated by fear of God and reparation for sin — and still be blind. Ignatius makes his powerful spiritual and psychological point: he was concerned "to achieve great deeds out of love for God," and do the same exercises of penance as did the saints of whom he read,

> if indeed not more. Such thoughts were his soul's only consolation: he had as yet no sense of inner values and did not understand what humility, love, and patience are. And he did not yet have that feeling for the will of God that he has to guide and moderate these virtues. (BDP, no. 14)

A cautionary tale, surely, and it inclines us to write in exclamatory style: How "crazy" the human soul can get! How easily can inhumanity be concealed "under the appearance of good"! How furiously aggressiveness can flash forth in the name of God's honor! And how sensitive this person has become in discerning what has taken place in him! How loving and humble is someone who makes his shaming experience available to himself and others as a learning experience! It is easy to find parallels in contemporary terrorism in the name of Allah, in the name of God, gods, and idols, party programs and ideology, which nevertheless insist that they seek only the best.

What was and would be the movement of conversion in the case of such warped behavior? For Ignatius, it was conversion from an "ego trip" to the "thou," to loving encounters. In loving encounters, the "I" need have no fear of coming up short. An expression of the ego trip were the fantasies of "mighty deeds" that "he" wished to accomplish. These were "his greatest consolation" — his "kicks," many would say today. Of consolations, joy, fulfillment in genuine encounter, "he" — Ignatius himself, then — had no sense as yet. He was blind.

Did Ignatius learn his lesson once and for all? Were there not further, perhaps more concealed and quieter motions of the soul reflecting something of an excessive sense of duty and a destructive aggressiveness? It is uncomfortable to read in his Book of the Exercises, "one should praise the bulls of the crusades." One wonders what moved the aging general to recommend the construction of a fleet to put the Turks, who were threatening the Mediterranean, in their place. Twenty years later came the Battle of Lepanto. Perhaps Ignatius had simply anticipated a concept that was strategically meaningful, geographically and culturally. But perplexing questions do still remain, especially the question of "humility, love, and patience."

In the First Letter to the Corinthians (12:31b–13:13), Paul writes that prophetical speech, a fiery passion for God, the sacrifice of one's life, giving away all of one's property, *without love*, are literally nothing. This shows how much human relationships and communication derive their value from humility, love, and patience. "Time is the school of love" (Hans Urs von Balthasar). Everything needs its time. Human beings need time to grow and mature. Developments and reforms in society and church need time. We ignore this at our peril. Patience is the basic attitude of living love in time. Patience is an elementary and basic prerequisite for communication. Everyday patience, then, is more than a mere everyday matter: "Patience is passion's deep breath" (E. Jüngel).

Reverence

Ignatius opens his autobiographical account with the statement that until the age of twenty-six he was primarily concerned with one thing: honor! Honor means recognition in the eyes of those who "have something to say." It means being a great success and being respected, being able to notice that one's own words count. A yearning to "be somebody," and not only for oneself, but also in the eyes of others, is doubtless as old as the human race. This yearning is not first and foremost pride, but is love for truth and life, love for one's own person. The person, the values of the human person, are unfathomably mysterious and great. One who grants this is honoring the truth. To honor someone means to attend to his or her worth. To honor means to allow a person to be great and to openly proclaim that she or he is great. Small-minded souls, vain egotists, upstarts driven by inferiority complexes, are incapable of allowing anyone but themselves to be great.

True, for Ignatius the drive to honor began to change with his conversion. But it took a long process of maturation before he could recognize, at the age of fifty-three, the fundamental attitude of "loving reverence" as the leitmotif of his life. "As I was saying Mass, I actually became convinced that I considered this grace and realization of the spiritual progress of my soul as more important than all of the graces bestowed upon me until then" (GT, 202). Ignatius characterizes this loving reverence in different ways:

1. Ignatius understands it not only as an occasional pleasant "impulse," but as a *way*. "Yes," he writes, "I gained the conviction that this is the way that the Lord wished to show me" (GT, 202). Reverence, here, is a kind of background coloration — an ever-present sign over all feeling, encounter, behavior, and communication. As a piece of music is written in a major or minor

key, so Ignatius's soul vibrates "in reverence" whatever it may be playing.

2. The development and growth of this basic spiritual attunement doesn't mean that it was primarily the result of strenuous asceticism. No, it was a *gift:* "I had found the way, then, that wished to show itself to me. It seemed to me that it was the best of all ways, and I must follow it forever" (GT, 205). A curious formula: "...that wished to show itself to me." Not a trail, then, that I simply blaze in the forest with a machete, but a way that comes to meet me, that "wishes to show itself to me." Almost a finding without seeking, and at the same time a strong invitation to follow this way "forever."

3. The characterization of reverence and the humility bound up with it, as a *loving reverence,* is important for Ignatius:

> Around this time it seemed to me that humility, reverence, and showing reverence ought to be not fearful, but loving, and this settled in my heart so powerfully that I repeatedly said, "But give me loving humility." And the same with respect and reverence, and I received new visitations with these words. (GT, 209)

This feeling echoes the Bible's declaration that "perfect love banishes fear." Ignatius sees, of course, altogether realistically, that there can be a reverence that is mixed with fear.

4. A further decisive step leads to the acknowledgment that reverence does not stop with God, to whom it is first directed. "It seems to me that this spirit would not stop there, but would also regard creatures, namely, loving humility and so forth" (GT, 209). *Human beings, the whole universe with its creatures,* are contemplated in loving reverence.

The art of communication means conducting encounters and conversations on the foundation of reverence. What is more precious than to be precious in the eyes of another? We must expand this statement: What is more precious than to be precious in the eyes of another's faith? Often enough, what first appears to our eyes concerning a person — perhaps even concerning our-

selves — is anything but precious. Despisers of persons can find
sufficient occasion for their resentments. How much that is imag-
ined, weak, hateful, lying, cowardly there is "in man"! And a
good psychologist can find much that is questionable underlying the noblest ideals, behaviors, and motives — or read it
into them.

Reverence for the "human being in the human being" is possible only when we see with the "eyes of the heart," as we read
in the Letter to the Ephesians. These eyes of the heart, the eyes
of faith, the eyes of love, the eyes of hope, can see the "pearl
in another's field," of which we hear in the parable. Those who
set their eyes on this pearl will not infrequently have the experience of really finding this pearl in another, even when the field
is outwardly overgrown or more resembles a dung-heap.

Reverence is a creative act. It can restore health to what has
seemed sick, dead, or lost, and bring it back to life. I think of a
young woman who had spent many years in the drug scene and
was the "nastiest of the nasty," even for herself. She recounted to
me what it meant for her to be hired as a babysitter by someone
who knew all about her — hired her "anyway." Reverence for
a person, faith in a person, can mean that that person will find
herself when she has believed herself lost.

Theologian, physician, and "jungle doctor" Albert Schweitzer
once said that only "reverence for life" can help guarantee the
oneness of the human being and the oneness of the religions.
Only reverence for the human being, the cosmos, animals, plants,
and stones, a reverence borne by love, can preserve creation.

Listening

"Since we are a conversation, we are..." One occasionally
comes across this phrase in belletristic works, where the encounter between human beings is called a conversation. Here
"encounter" means not just that people are talking with one
another, but that in their relationship the persons themselves
are, as it were, a conversation. We almost never hear the com-

plete phrase, "Since we are a conversation and can listen to each other. . . . "

Few words, in our time, enjoy such high appreciation as "listen" and "be able to listen." This is surely a sign that real "listening" and "the ability to listen" are felt as a commodity that are in short supply, and therefore earnestly sought after. We even read, occasionally, in the classified section of the paper, that someone wants to "rent" a person for an hour of listening. Listening, for men and women as communicative creatures, is as air for breathing and space for meeting. In *Momo,* Michael Ende's children's novel for adults that became a cult-classic in Germany some years ago, little Momo stands out because of her gift for listening. Through listening, she awakens life in human beings.

I think of the psychotherapist who said that once he finds that a patient can listen again, he believes the person has been cured. Normally one of the crucial things in therapy is the patient's coming to self-expression. This is an important step, and it bespeaks an increase of trust. But just speaking can become monologuing, and leave persons stuck in their own delusions, self-analyses, and ego-excesses. In listening, the opening to the "thou" occurs, and real communication begins.

Mental or emotional diseases can usually be described as communication diseases, or based on difficulties of communication. The ability to listen, and the openness to another's words are signs of healing. The ability to speak that comes from listening, and listening that is oriented to another's words, constitute redeemed conversation. This makes it clear that listening is a highly "active phenomenon." Hearing and listening do not mean apathetically and passively letting something fly past one's ears. They constitute a turning to someone in fellow feeling, a sympathetic shared experience, an assimilation, an understanding, a digesting of what has been heard.

Listening can also mean, often enough, having patience. It is reported of Ignatius, by a member of his house community: "It is also remarkable, with what great patience he listens to useless things from "externs" [the technical Jesuit term for outsiders] and even long, drawn-out speeches from those in the house. He hears them out, then replies" (MEVI, no. 202).

German President Roman Herzog, in his Christmas address of 1995, said things about conversation, especially about listening, that could scarcely be more impressive:

> Often it is enough merely to listen to a lonely, withdrawn person. I know that great patience is required now and then, even tolerance. After all, a great deal of loneliness can be traced back to the shortcomings of the person who is lonely. But such patience is usually worth it: gradually the conversation partner opens up and rewards you with growing trust, even with friendship. And besides — even when that does not happen — any conversation in which you don't do all the talking, but simply listen, can lead to an endless amount of learning and experience. In my job, I can see this from the opposite side. How often would I like to just take part in a function and listen to the persons. But then the participants inundate me with requests to say something on the subject, and if possible, something that will afford guidance to my hearers. But how am I supposed to have ideas that point the way when I have not been allowed to hear the cares and problems of the participant first? I advise you: Don't be roped into this game! Listen, before you judge. I shall carve out this free space for myself, again. (Herzog, 1995, 1085)

To add anything to words like these would be overkill. It will be enough carefully to note them.

Trust

Trust is another basic premise for communication. Trust is to communication what earth is to plants: there is no other place to strike root. There is nothing worse than when one faces a wall of mistrust.

I remember a communications interplay one weekend at which one visiting job-seeker did not know that another applicant had already been hired and that his application would be rejected whatever he said. The conversation itself, and the evaluation, produced this result: it was a terrible ordeal for the candidate constantly to feel a wall of unexpressed rejection. Regardless of what he said, or what the others had to say in seeming friendliness and encouragement, an atmosphere of rejection and mistrust reigned supreme.

What an experience it is, on the other hand, when you meet someone who gives you trust "on credit," pays you a "communications credit," so to speak, that declares: "Pending certification to the contrary, I trust you." And how do you feel in the opposite case, when your correspondent says, expressly or by implication, "I basically don't trust you. You must constantly prove yourself and your credibility."

Trust is a crucial part of the equipment, so to speak, of those in positions of leadership and direction. If they have no trust in others, they produce nothing great. They have to take personal charge of everything, and they groan in desperation, "Why do I have to do everything myself?" — meaning, it would indeed be better to do it all myself, but, unfortunately, this is impossible.

There is a classic example of the great trust that Ignatius had in his confreres. It will be worthwhile to relish it in all detail. Father da Câmara tells the story:

> I remember how he took care to summon a Father whom he was sending to deal on affairs of great importance with important persons from Rome, and he told him "Come here. I want you to go and handle this matter with Cardinal So-and-So, and I want you to take care of it. My aim is such and such, and the following means have been made available to me." And after he had given him all of the necessary information and instruction, he added: "But I want you to apply the means that the Lord instructs you

are most suitable, and I leave you all freedom to do what
seems best to you." At times he behaved in this manner
with me; and when I returned in the evening, the first thing
he asked me was: "Are you happy with yourself?" He took
it for granted that I had handled the matter in all freedom,
and that everything I had done originated with me. (MEVI,
no. 269)

We often hear of the so-called "work environment." What
work environment flourishes where supervisors like Ignatius deal
with their fellow workers? Clearly spelled out arrangements for
achieving goals, helpful indications of possible ways and means,
and an equally clear commission that gives the agent a free hand:
"You must see on the spot what is advisable in the concrete
situation in order to gain the end we have in view." In this kind
of work relationship, attention to the person and that person's
freedom, trust, and the capacity to delegate, play a decisive role.
Surely there is also an evaluation, but what a pleasant way to
open such a "check-up conversation" with the words, "Are you
happy with yourself?"

Ignatius once gave a man who had entered the Society of Jesus
only one year before "a large number of sheets of paper, all blank
except for Ignatius's signature at the bottom of each. Depending
on what he judged appropriate, he was to write documents or
letters on them to whomever and however he wished." This story
of the "blank checks" receives an explanation: "Detailed instructions *were* supplied for everything, along with suggestions to be
put to use in this or that situation, but there was no obligation
to go this way or any other — none whatever."

Not only in an intimate "one-on-one," but also in a larger
context, trust is a premise for communication. In politics, there
are what are called "trust-building measures": for example,
when one state, at least a little distance away, unilaterally dis-
arms, and therewith sends a signal. A conscious surrender of
small advantages can eventually gain great advantages for all
involved. On the level of economics, there is such a thing as

a credit. True, the recipient's "credit-worthiness" is carefully checked, but the lending institution often enough runs a risk. Credit belongs to the creed of the economy. And trust belongs to the creed of every communication.

Attention to One's Neighbor's Difference

For Ignatius, it pertains to the ABCs of communication to pay close attention to a person's character and to the various life situations in which people find themselves, and to react to these things appropriately.

There is a certain humor in the way Ignatius, when he writes a letter to some confreres headed for Ireland, talks about heeding the temperament and character of their opposite numbers. Generally the Irish have a reputation for hot-headedness, and so the indications for dealing with "choleric" persons may well have been framed with them especially in mind. The corresponding instruction, "On the Art and Manner of Work and Communication with Persons in the Lord," of September 1541 belongs to the key texts on the Ignatian art of communication. After enjoining all possible brevity in conversations, Ignatius speaks in somewhat greater detail about taking the character of one's conversation partner into account.

> With an eye to dealing with some important persons, or with those in authority, and obtaining their love for greater service to God our Lord, one should first see what kind of person he is dealing with, and adapt oneself accordingly — namely, if he is choleric and quick, and speaks in a lively manner, somehow, in the conversation regarding good and holy things, adopt his manner, and show oneself not grave, phlegmatic, or melancholic. With those who by nature are reserved, slow in their speech, earnest and weighty in their conversation, adopt their manner with regard to them. For it is this that they find comfortable: "I have become all things to all men" (1 Cor. 9:22).

One point to be observed: When someone is of a choleric disposition and is dealing with another choleric person, and they are not both of the same mind, there is very great danger of a clash in their words when they hold conversation. Therefore when someone recognizes that he himself is of a choleric disposition, even in small details when dealing with others, that one, when possible, ought to go armed with an examination of conscience, or some other reminder, in order to suffer and not be provoked by others, especially when he knows that the other is ill. When he speaks with a phlegmatic or melancholic person, there is no great danger of their quarreling because of over-hasty words. (BU, 63)

Regardless of how we may judge the four "humors" of sanguinic, melancholic, choleric, and phlegmatic, which have come down from antiquity, Ignatius's reference shows one thing: he thinks it helpful to have a grasp of a person's peculiar features. It seems to have been his experience that people typically react in certain basic ways and that it is prudent to take them into account. We may bracket the question of whether Ignatius would have adopted today, instead, the categories of Carl Jung, who speaks of introverted and extroverted persons, or the system of the four basic forms of fear, as Fritz Riemann has them. Perhaps — just perhaps — he would have taken a course with the Jesuits in the United States, who in the 1980s, made the enneagram and its theory of character-types popular all over the world. In any case, it is clear that a sense of basic attitudes, basic motivations, intentions, peculiarities, preferences, and fears in one's conversation partner, belongs to the ABCs of the Ignatian practice of communication.

The reason is simply that he takes the other as other, the particular person in question, seriously, just as he is. It matters whether someone in a encounter is preponderantly governed by the will to help or the will to success, the will to idiosyncrasy, knowledge, adaptation, optimism, striving for power, perfection, and so on (this is the direction taken by the characterizations of the enneagrams). To see this, and to deal with it flexibly, requires a great deal of experience and circumspection.

It is also especially important and helpful to attend to the psychic and somatic disposition of one's particular conversation partner. Ignatius here cites the example of that partner's state of health. He could just as well have cited social position, economic and professional situation, the mood of the moment, and so on. It makes a difference whether someone has just lost his wife or is newly married, whether someone has "hit the jackpot" or lost everything gambling. Each situation, be it a person's disposition or outer circumstances, is always to be taken into account when there is question of communication.

Telling the Truth in Love: "Entering by the Other's Door"

The formulation that one should "enter by the door of the other" is adequate to demonstrate the essentials of Ignatian communication, even though it is a Spanish proverb and not Ignatius's invention.

When I seek access to another, it is sensible to look at where the other is open. A head running into a wall is not the best door opener. The finger lightly tapping wins access more easily than the fist banging on the door. In today's pastoral and social work, the formula goes "Meet others where they are!" And if they are standing in the rain, then I have to go there — not leave them standing there, however, but try to take them to a dry place. The point is that Ignatius certainly has goals in mind. For him, the basic sense of a helping encounter always stood, as he put it, "to help souls," to assist human beings to salvation. This could certainly mean that he would listen long and patiently to someone's endless round of war-stories, only to make a gentle transition to the question of the inner, spiritual fight for life. At times some of his interlocutors must have been surprised to see where the conversation wound up. Someone who had begun with laments over the bad old days of war or with a feeling of triumph at the victory of his own party suddenly saw himself confronted with the battles being waged in his own soul and the good and evil spirits at work in his heart. All that was left now was for Ignatius to tell him to make the Exercises for eight days! This, too, belonged to the pastoral prudence of the sometime defender of the Fort of Pamplona. Ignatius knew a thing or two about war, about open and weak points, as a remark from the Book of the Exercises testifies (see GU, no. 327).

That the "prudent encounter" is a tight-rope walk is perhaps shown by the very fact that Ignatius in his words about the doors points to the devil, who commonly begins with good and pious thoughts, thereupon seducing the soul to evil gradually, under the appearance of good. Ignatius continues: "In this way, we can praise what is good in a people, or agree with them in a single good matter, while we pass over the things that are bad with them. And since we win their love, we succeed better in our affairs. And while we go in by their door, we come out by our own" (BU, 63–64).

With language like this, we must repeatedly hold our breath. We recognize the abiding true message when we understand the images in their plain sense: One should enter by the door of another, and not, at the first confrontation or meeting, immediately knock the door down. Anyone looking for a still more unambiguous statement and seeking to absolve Ignatius of false motives, ought to read a letter, whose exact date we don't know, to young students at Alcalá. It is one of the key Ignatian texts on the art of communication: "One of the things in which we must ground ourselves, in order to please our Lord, will consist in this, that we repudiate all things that can separate us from love for the brethren, while we make an effort to love them with the love of our heart. For the highest wisdom says: 'By this shall all know that you are my disciples' (John 13:35)" (BU, 935–36).

What Ignatius understands by pastoral communication and pastoral motivation for conversations can scarcely be put more clearly. For Ignatius, what "motivates insight" in "control-free communication" is love. Nowhere is this expressed more beautifully than in the Paul's Letter to the Ephesians: "But speaking the truth in love, we must grow up in every way into him who is the head, into Christ" (Eph. 4:15). Here everything is found together in one sentence: love, truth, the phenomenon of growth, and the goal: life in Christ.

For Ignatius, this signpost is valid even for the conflict-charged dialogue with the Protestants. He very clearly supported the cause of the Counter-Reformation. And one can find quotations from Ignatius that, nowadays at least, have no good solutions to offer for ecumenical encounters. But there are far more passages in letters of Ignatius that invite persons to a loving contact, passages inspired by the fact that the reform of one's own life is the best preaching and best foundation for conversation.

One man who assimilated these instructions for encounter on the deepest level is Peter Canisius, the great figure of the Catholic Reform in Germany. Although often vehemently abused and vituperated, he sought to have reconciling encounters. We have an eloquent testimonial in a letter he wrote to a professor of theology at Dillingen. Peter shares the latter's basic view, but not his tone:

A number of learned men are of the same view as I, that you ought to select a less harsh tone, in your writings, in many places, especially when you pun on the names of Calvin, Melanchthon, and other persons of this kind. This sort of crass word-play is the style of popular speakers, but not of theologians nowadays. Nor, if we use such medicines, will we ever heal those who have fallen ill, but only make their condition hopeless.... Therefore you should afford German readers no kind of pretext to fault, in this writing and in your other works, the overzealousness of a beginner. Rather they should feel a certain dignity and mildness, appropriate for a theologian, and feel attracted by it. This deserves attention especially for your communication with the bishops. The thing to do is to combine zeal with Christian prudence, in order, in these so dangerous times and circumstances for the church, not to tear down instead of building up. (Canisius, 181–82).

Had there been more "reconciling Christian persons" like Canisius and Philip Melanchthon on both sides, perhaps one of the darkest chapters in church history on excommunication would not have had to be written.

Chapter 4

Exercises

"Getting Lucky" with Spiritual Communication

The Spiritual Exercises are no doubt a preferred site for Ignatian communication. Swayed by its many pointers for meditation, and biblical contemplation, people have hitherto grossly undervalued this feature of the Exercises. When we think about the efficacy of the Exercises, we shall certainly need to speak of the Holy Spirit's work of grace. Surely Ignatius's spiritual experiences and his fine spiritual and psychological touch are part of the Exercises' "secret of success." But also "responsible" for the effectiveness of the Exercises is the fact that they offer not only helps for prayer, for meditation, but are an extraordinary stockpile of communication material, an extraordinary communication process.

By way of a series of rhetorical questions: Where has there ever been, in Christian pastoral theory and practice, the opportunity to carry on a conversation for a week? Where is there a safe place in which the whole history of one's life, with its peaks and valleys, can be discussed? Where can people come to terms with all the ambiguity and guilt of their lives? Where are people with their questions about meaning, with their search for God, not all alone on the way but together with a guide?

We could go on with this type of question. Today as well, when we seem fairly showered with offers of counsel and guidance, intensive, individual, and personal conversation about faith and life is nevertheless a rare experience for most Christians. Even group conversations on faith are more the exception

61

than the rule. And when we look back into the history of the church, then, it is true, we find "leaders of souls" here and there, but their benefit was reserved primarily for Christians in cloisters, for priests and nuns. This "offer of expert conversation" to ordinary lay people making the Exercises individually with a spiritual director (and this was the original method) remains something unique.

In Ignatius's Book of the Exercises, we find a whole series of annotations that relate directly to conversation between, literally, the one "who gives the Exercises" and the one "who receives the Exercises." However reticent they may be in tone and content, in their brevity and conciseness they are powerful statements and show Ignatius to be a "master of communication."

Basic Statements on Spiritual Direction

Ignatius makes certain statements that set forth, as it were, the "first principle and foundation" of any spiritual direction. On this basis rest all further declarations.

1. Mutual Receiving and Giving

Ignatius never speaks of the "retreat master," or of even the "companion for the Exercises," but speaks altogether pragmatically of "the one who gives the Exercises" and "the one who receives them." The usual translation, "who makes the Exercises," is not exact. In the original text, the reading is, "who receives the Exercises" (GU, no. 22). Thus, one does not "make" the Exercises; one receives them. And so even the choice of words indicates a situation in which persons give and receive. Encounter lives on giving and receiving.

Here we must emphasize that a *mutual* giving and receiving occurs. This is clear in the words of the famous "Preliminary Observation" in the Book of the Exercises: "That both the giver and the receiver of the Spiritual Exercises may be of greater help and benefit to each other…" (GU, no. 22). It is not the case, then, that the one is rich and gives, while the other is poor and receives. Both — in their respective ways sharing the Exercises — receive and bestow.

The so-called service professions — whether social work or the various methods of psychotherapy and counseling — have for many years looked for ways to frame the relationship of therapist and client, of the one who helps and the one who receives help. Behind the questioning lurks the malaise that the way roles are assigned to physician and patient, therapist or counselor and client, is at times inadequate. How can we avoid one side's playing the part of the omniscient helper, while the person on the couch plays the poor, sick, helpless, weak patient? To be sure, there is a distinction of roles in this phenomenon of assistance, and there must be. But how can we make sure that this does not lead to a fixed alternation in which the one helping is, so to say, always the "heavyweight," and the patient floats in the air as the lightweight? Ignatius's experience, on which he has reflected, gives a direction. Obviously, for him, as a highly experienced adviser, he has repeatedly found that both parties are a "help and benefit" to each other. And this is indeed the experience of many who work with the Exercises, that both sides feel they have been the beneficiaries.

Of course, there is also a role-differentiation in the Exercises that is important for the counseling process. But the basis for the encounter is the personal, brotherly-sisterly equality of the children of God. They meet each other in free bestowal *and* reception, in being poor *and* being rich. This is Ignatius's experience, and he makes it the "Principle and Foundation" of any spiritual advising.

2. The Foundation of Trust and Understanding

In the so-called Preamble of the Exercises, Ignatius speaks about what he considers a presupposition: "that every good Christian ought to be more eager to put a good interpretation on a neigh-

bor's statement than to condemn it." What an invitation, right
at the beginning of the Exercises, to an encounter free of prejudice! It must not be my first concern to justify my statements.
I need not be afraid that I am talking nonsense, or that what
I'm proposing is completely stupid for sure. I need not begin by
making excuses for what I'm saying. I need not fear that my
neighbor is on the watch to throw my words back in my face.
The person advising me is good and well-disposed toward me
and tries to "save" my statements.

This consciousness lies at the origin of trust, and trust facilitates an ever deeper understanding. What is more beneficial than
to have the feeling that here is someone listening to me, and not
only outwardly, but understanding me from the inside in such
a way that I understand myself better? What greater "help to
development" can there be than when someone entertains such
a "positive judgment"? A classic biblical example for a negative and a positive judgment is the encounter between Nathanael
and Jesus in John 1:43–51. Nathanael's first reaction is, "Can
anything good come out of Nazareth?" And Jesus' reaction, by
contrast, is "Behold, an Israelite indeed, in whom there is no
guile!..." The "positive judgment" has its effect: Jesus opens
Nathanael for his encounter with him: "Rabbi, you are the Son
of God!"

Trust and understanding are basic to the Exercises. Here are
grounds for why, normally, before the Exercises, a rather lengthy
preliminary conversation takes place, that adviser and advisee
may experience whether it's "going to go." During the Exercises
themselves it will be important to immediately address possible
troubles or to check when the one or the other has the impression
of not having rightly understood something.

3. The Divine "Triangular Relation"

The expression "triangular relationship" usually designates a
difficult situation: one marriage partner is involved in an affair
with a third person, and now the original two-party relationship

can be disturbed or even destroyed. Ignatius writes of a triangular relationship that is one of the fundamental prerequisites for the success of a spiritual relationship: the advising of a person and that person's allowing himself or herself to be advised always takes place in the presence of God. God is so much the "actual partner" that Ignatius can say that the one giving the Exercises should, "more like a scale poised in the middle, let the Creator work immediately with the creature, and the creature with his or her Creator and Lord" (GU, no. 15).

This can be illustrated with an example: In marriage counseling, for example, it is of decisive importance that the therapist not smuggle himself into the role of a partner, or offer himself as a partner substitute, so that the therapy degenerates into a failed therapist-client relationship. Both partners must bear in mind that what's at stake here is the healing of the couple's actual relationship. The other partner must, so to speak, always be invisibly present. In this sense it should always be the concern in spiritual counseling that the actual relationship grow and succeed. To put it in another way: The adviser leaves the advisee to God's guidance, to his hand, his Spirit. The adviser is present only to help the advisee to see, to indicate stumbling blocks, to encourage, to make comments.

4. Communion of Love and Life with God in All Things

The goal is crucial for any path and so too for guidance along a path. The obvious "goal" of the Exercises — if it can be at all appropriate to speak in the rather functional language of ends and means — for the one who gives them and the one who receives them is "that the Creator and Lord himself may communicate himself to the devout soul, embracing it with love, inciting it to praise of himself, and disposing it for the way which will most enable the soul to serve him in the future" (GU, no. 15).

This text may be seen as still warmer and more eloquent if we look at it in its original form, where we read that God "clasps" a person, "embraces" that person "in order that he or she attain love." "Contact, embrace, are to awaken love for total surrender." Ignatius is ultimately concerned, with regard to the one who "receives" the Exercises, with only one thing, the "one thing necessary": sharing, self-sharing, and help in case of "disturbances in communication."

Typically, in the Spanish text, the word *comunicar* is again used for "share": "Criador y Señor se communique a la su anima devota" — "The Creator and Lord ... should communicate himself to the devout soul" (GU, no. 15). The response to God's word and touch is given with one's whole life, with one's whole heart, with all of one's powers.

Basic Attitudes on the Part of the Adviser

"The tone makes the music," not only in music, but also in conversation, in the process of counseling. The tone becomes a "good tone" when the inner positions and attitudes can be heard in it that are important for good communication. Without such inner resonance one's conversation partner quickly picks up on what are just word-games and techniques learned by rote. Some of the important basic attitudes for conversation have been presented in detail in Chapter Three. In the section that follows, they will be presented from the standpoint of the Exercises.

1. Attentive Listening, Cautious and Gentle Speech

Ignatius described the attitude of attentive hearing and careful speech in his letter to his three confreres who had been sent to the Council of Trent as simply and clearly as can be: "In your place I should be slow, reflective, affectionate in speech.... Again, I should be slow in speech, and should seek to learn as I listened." Listening can even pass over into a kind of *contemplative listening*. Of course, one must continue to be attentive to the words that someone speaks. The center of attentiveness, however, is directed toward the person as a whole. The words flow past more like leaves on a stream, while the one meditating them

pays close attention. And in this "meditating attention," something can appear as important entirely spontaneously, "entirely
of itself." Thus, it is more a matter of a person-centered listening
than of strenuous attention to each word, with reflection on and
analysis of it in the act of listening.

This ground rule of attentive listening is valid for each of the
daily conversations of the Exercises. It shows its importance also
in the observation for the one who gives the Exercises, to the
effect that the indications for the meditation should be "brief."
Ignatius gives the reason for this:

> For then the one who is making the contemplation, by
> reviewing the true essentials of the subject, and by per-
> sonal reflection and reasoning may find something that will
> make it a little more meaningful to him or touch him more
> deeply...This is a greater spiritual satisfaction and pro-
> duces more fruit than if the one who is giving the Exercises
> were to discourse at great length and amplify the meaning
> of the subject matter, for it is not the abundance of knowl-
> edge that fills and satisfies the soul, but rather an interior
> understanding and savoring of things. (GU, no. 2).

It is not a matter, then, of the adviser's drumming his collected
knowledge into the exercitant's head. Rather it is a matter of the
adviser's feeling what the exercitant needs and then making a
brief indication that will send the latter down the road of his or
her own discovery.

An experience that a religious sister recounted to me may
make the importance of listening clear. She was visiting an old
sister of her order. The two had long been friends, and the old sister was at the point of death. Since she knew that this was likely
their last visit together, she was especially open to every word
the grievously ill sister said. "Would you like to say something
more?" asked the visitor. And the answer came, "Unless you're
here, you don't hear it." Somewhat surprised at the response, the
younger sister asked what her friend had meant. But the other
only said, peacefully and with her own emphasis, "Unless you're

entirely here, you don't hear *it*." And that was all. A deep word for contemplative hearing and digesting: being completely there, in order to hear.

2. One's Own Freedom Liberates the Other

The First Principle and Foundation of the Exercises includes the attitude of "indifference" (see GU, no. 23), the "freedom of the spirit," that is to grow more and more in the course of the Exercises. This is valid not only for the one receiving the Exercises, but also for the one giving them: "The one giving the Exercises should not urge the one receiving them toward poverty or any other promise more than toward their opposites, or to one state of life more than to another" (GU, no. 15).

This is, so to speak, the royal charter, the charter that must define the relationship of advising. The adviser must be in a state of equilibrium "like a scale" — not like a weight loaded onto the scale! No matter how happy the one giving the Exercises might be to see a hopeful young man enter his own order, he is not to get involved. The Exercises were not meant as a recruiting campaign! They were primarily intended to help the exercitants to become free, in order to hear the call of the Spirit of God and to follow it of their own free will.

It would be just as inappropriate and would diminish the freedom of the encounter, if one asked piercing, penetrating questions in order to "sort someone out and get to know them" (see GU, no. 17) — although "it is very advantageous for the director to be faithfully informed about the various agitations and thoughts which the different spirits stir up in the retreatant" (ibid.). It is also a matter of allowing the growth of a space for trust and listening, in which those receiving the Exercises feel free to express themselves, to unburden themselves, perhaps to weep and to make a crucial admission. As for the one giving the Exercises: listen without interrogating, listen without eviscerating.

It is important, then, that the adviser himself or herself

continually grow into the attitude of indifference, into the "attentiveness in free suspension" that follows the movements of the way of prayer and heart of the exercitant. The inner freedom of the adviser is found at the point where passivity and activity, trust and effort, letting go and getting busy, intersect. One must be entirely reliant on the activity of God's Spirit, as if one must and could do nothing at all oneself, and yet be "entirely there," as if one's own presence were of decisive importance.

3. Attention to the Particularity of the Individual

Closely bound up with the requirement of granting space for freedom is the attitude of attention to the particularity of each individual person: "The Spiritual Exercises should be adapted to the disposition of the persons who desire to make them, that is, to their age, education, and ability" (GU, no. 18). This instruction for the adviser is further spelled out by Ignatius in numerous ways: The posture, in prayer, should shift, according to whatever is best for the one at prayer: kneeling, sitting, or lying down; the exercitants are to remain in the position that most helps them on their way; the steps in the way are to be shortened or prolonged, whichever is necessary; the instructions for prayer should be short, so that the individual may independently reflect and have the opportunity to digest the material.

The way Ignatius set up the one-on-one conversation is the best testimonial to what he knows from experience: apart from the sermon, which is spoken to all, there must be another help more suited to the character, the manner of life, and the various experiences of the different individuals.

4. Advising in Conjunction with God

Ignatius often speaks of our service of God as that of an *instrumentum conjunctum,* that is, as that of a tool connected with God. Again and again he stresses that one should use all "natural means," such as good sense, rules for communication, and

so on, but he emphasizes that the decisive thing is inner connection with God. Like the brush in the hand of the painter,
like the shepherd's flute, like the oil in the hand of the Good
Samaritan, so should the adviser be "God's pencil" (Mother
Teresa). Advisers should allow themselves to be taken completely into service and pursue no interests of their own. Only
thus can one truly serve another. And only thus do service and
encounter materialize out of an attitude of "committed composure" (Teilhard de Chardin), which is fully engaged and yet
awaits everything.

5. Advising with a Pure Intention

"But we only wanted what was best for you!" How often parents say this when they have perhaps learned too late that,
in spite of their good intentions, they have not always served
their children's best interests. And perhaps the rejoinder — "No,
you're not going to get what's best for me!" — is more than
simply being smart-alecky. Perhaps the response expresses the
fact that what is best for a person is very often not what others
think it is. Certainly the adage, "The opposite of 'well' is 'well-
meant' " is a caricature of the actual "good intention," but there
is much truth in it as well. The pure, truly loving intention always wishes what is really the best for others — but it does not
seek to force it on them; rather it seeks to give them the help
of counseling, so that the "best" may come into being from
within them.

   In this connection, it may be significant to recall that when
Jesus met people, he occasionally asked them, "What do you
wish? What do you want me to do for you?" He does this even
in situations in which one might ask in puzzlement, "Now, what
kind of question is that? Isn't it clear that this sick person wants
to be healed?" But it was obviously very important for Jesus
that the people he met discover for themselves and express what
they really want. The question awakens in a person the power

of will, the power of faith, the power of hope, the potency of longing.

6. Encounter in Love

Just as the commandment of the love of God and neighbor contains "the whole law," so also does love embrace the whole law of counseling. Peter Faber, of whom Ignatius says that he could probably give the Exercises better than anyone else, since he had imbibed their spirit, writes to Peter Canisius instructions for the apostolate among the Protestants (in the language of his time): "The first thing is: one who would help the heretics of our time must see to it that he meet them with great love, and that he loves them in truth, and deliver his spirit from all considerations that could be detrimental to respect for them" (Faber, 374). What a respectful instruction, in a time when it was customary to abuse one another in the very worst way!

By no means does love mean simply approving everything. Real love knows necessary, liberating confrontation, as well, but this is always in order "to correct the person with love" and to seek every appropriate means through which a person "might arrive at the correct understanding and thus save himself" (GU, no. 22). The point is not to impose alien and alienating standards from without, but to cooperate and help, in order that the Spirit, who speaks in everyone with "inexpressible words," may indeed utter a word.

Only when the one giving the Exercises is at the same time an outer, human representative of the great inward "con-*front*-ation," does the encounter occur that is one of the most precious gifts of the Exercises: meeting "face to face."

Basic Perspectives of Advising

Granted, the one giving the Exercises must attend to a great deal, and to a great many details, in the process of advising. But Ignatius has certain basic perspectives, certain decisive viewpoints, which he never lets disappear from view.

1. The "Stirrings" and "Motions"

Ignatius's chief concern when it comes to the conversation of advising is the question of interior stirrings and motions. The Exercises are not performed on the level of a theological-spiritual exchange of thoughts. It is a matter of the stirrings and motions of the heart. In Holy Scripture, these come to expression primarily in connection with the fruits of the Spirit and the operation of the Enemy. Such movements are peace, restlessness, ease, freedom, clarity, agreeableness, fear, inhibition, inner compulsions, hatred, ambition, feelings of inferiority, and so on.

A key biblical example of attention to movements of the heart is to be found in Mary: "But Mary treasured all these words and pondered them in her heart" (Luke 2:19). What we have, then, are movements, motions, and experiences in the interior of a person. Here we must attend to the fact that these experiences are not simply identical with the emotions and feelings. Motions can be very gentle, very quiet, and yet very deep and transforming. To be sure, they can be loud, so to speak, and dramatic. But frequently it is a matter of touches that are as gentle and quiet as Mary's being touched by the Spirit of God: "The power of the Most High will *overshadow* you" (see Luke 1:26–38).

Precisely here it is the function of the one giving the Exercises to call attention to what is quiet, to what is easily overlooked or not really heard. God does not always speak in emotional earthquakes; sometimes — as with Elijah — it is in the breath of the breeze. The Spirit of God often speaks without a "noise of words," as Ignatius once formulated it.

2. Help in the "Discernment of Spirits"

Why must the Exercises be "given"? What is the function of the one accompanying the exercitant? The answer can be summed up very briefly: to help in the discernment of spirits. Some one-third of the twenty instructions at the beginning of the Exercises and a whole series of rules (see GU, nos. 313–36) deal expressly with the discernment of spirits. Here the decisive question arises: "In which direction do the 'stirrings and motions' lead? In the direction of the Spirit of God, whose fruits are faith, hope, love, liberty, truth, humility, patience, peace, joy, and so on? Or in the direction of the evil spirit, whose fruits are mistrust, resignation, lovelessness, egotism, unfreedom, lies, rage, hatred, jealousy, and so on?

Surely those making the Exercises must feel the discernment from within and seek to find it themselves. But here the saying especially holds true, that four eyes see more than two. Those giving the Exercises cannot and need not open and heal blind eyes, but they can give "helps to see."

3. Counseling at Various Stages of the Journey

Closely bound up with the discernment of spirits is the necessity that the one giving the Exercises take cognizance of the various stages of the way of the Exercises. Just as the service of accompanying someone takes on a different aspect depending on whether the journey is through the countryside or in the city, whether it is a journey through the wilderness or "over green meadows," so is it also with the spiritual way: whether we seek the "first principle and foundation" of our life, or experience guilt and a reconciling redemption, whether we know we have been called to the way of discipleship, whether we are discovering a mission for our life, whether we stand at the cross or would flee it, whether we "have died and are risen with Christ" — these are altogether distinct spiritual landscapes for the pilgrim of the Exercises. On each spiritual "leg of the journey," different events occur: everything at one stage of the way occurs under a different omen, the "spirits" are different, temptations are different, and it is important to sort out all of these differences as part of the advising process.

We have an example of the necessity of a feel for the particular "legs of the journey," that is, of the "weeks" in the Exercises, for example, in Ignatius's declaration: "To the same extent that the rules of the First Week will help a person, those of the Second Week will be harmful" when the course of the Exercises is still in the stage of the First Week (GU, no. 9). What is poison for one condition can be medicine in another situation. What is a help to one person can injure someone who is "in another week." What is for one a necessary awakening of conscience, in another situation may be scrupulosity, and this to the point of suicidal thoughts, as happened with Ignatius himself. When someone comes to the point of accepting and repeating a yes to life, God's yes to life in gratitude, it can be really misleading to speak of renunciation and the way of the cross. Or just the other way around, someone may get no further in love and life unless that person is ready to integrate darkness, pain, emptiness, loneliness, perseverance in the darkness of faith, and thus to grow in depth. There is no end to the list of occasions for recognition and discernment.

4. The Process of the Exercises

The concept of "holism" is one of the spiritual words in fashion today, and one wishes it a long life. Holism means that the whole human being sets off down the road — with skin and hair, brains and heart, with thoughts and experiences, with an entire life history — with body, soul, and spirit.

In the letter already mentioned, to the Jesuit conciliar theologians, Ignatius describes this notion in the form of a fundamental directive for conversation. He would seek "to grasp the thoughts, feelings, and intentions of the speakers." Saying that attention should be paid to the thoughts, feelings, and intentions of the speaker makes it clear that Ignatius has the entire person in view. Indeed the multiplicity of opportunities for exercise shows how holistic the process of the Exercises is: it engages fantasy, images, stories, life stories, various bodily dispositions, all bod-

ily and spiritual senses, feelings, movements — the deepest heart
and personal core of a human being. Just as Ignatius says that
God should be sought and found in everything, so could one
say that one should pray with all of the forces that make up the
human person.

5. Attending to External Circumstances: The "Setting"

Not only are inner stirrings and motions of importance, but
external circumstances and conditions are to be attended to,
as well — what psychology calls the "setting." To these exter-
nals belong one's space, the climate, nourishment, the seasons,
sleep, the rules of encounter, one's schedule, and so on. Apposite instructions for everything are found in the Book of the
Exercises.

Ignatius's notes are so varied and differentiated that we must
express the warning once more — not for Ignatius himself but
for "people like ourselves" — not to seek to assure the success
of the Exercises by applying his methods too much. Here too, as
with the process of the Exercises across the board, a glance at
Mary can help, especially in the scene of the Annunciation (see
Luke 1:26–38). She answers the announcement that God's love
is in her and seeks to take form, not with the question, "What
shall I now do?" but "How can this be?" In the same way, it
could be more appropriate sometimes to say, "I should like to
let the Exercises happen," instead of, in a spirit of activism, "I
am doing the Spiritual Exercises."

Concrete "Interventions"

Ignatius gives not only general instructions for basic attitudes on
the part of the one who gives the Exercises, but also instructions
for concrete interventions for the behavior of the one receiving
the Exercises. When and how should the person who gives the
Exercises "intervene," react, respond?

1. "Let the Instructions Be Brief"

Exercises in the form of talks, especially when they leave room for meditation, surely have their place. But for the original form of Ignatian Exercises, for the individual Exercises, we read: Let the instructions for the meditation be given "with only a brief or summary explanation" (GU, no. 2). Symbolically speaking, the one giving the Exercises may and should cut a decent slice from the loaf of bread and hand it to the exercitant, but he should not spoon-feed him!

2. Encouragement to Perseverance and Progress

Ignatius obviously often had the experience of someone becoming disheartened in the Exercises after running into hard times. When the giver of the Exercises sees that the exercitant is experiencing desolation and temptation, the giver should not treat the retreatant severely or harshly, but gently and kindly. The director should encourage and strengthen the exercitant for the future (GU, no. 7). The one giving the Exercises should support and encourage the exercitant to "stick it out" to the end of the time set for the meditation (see GU, nos. 12–13).

3. Questioning the Exercitant after the Course of the Exercises

Extensive as is Ignatius's experience with dry times for the soul, he is just as extensively convinced that, in the long run, something in the exercitant will "get going," if the exercitant perseveres along the proposed way. So he stops the adviser at this point:

> When the one giving the Exercises notices that the person making them is not experiencing any spiritual motions in his or her soul, such as consolation or desolation, or is not being moved one way or another by different spirits, the director should question the exercitant carefully about the Exercises: whether the exercitant is making them at the appointed

times, how they are being made, and whether the Additional
Directives are being diligently observed. The director should
ask about each of these three items in particular. (GU, no. 6)

Ignatius has no false timidity when it comes to speaking of the
"contract of the Exercises." Of course, it's crucial whether the
questioning takes place in the harsh tone of a schoolmaster or in
an atmosphere of free speech and sensitive help and counseling.

4. Helping to Convey Insights

Seeing and insight must be matters for the individual. But it is
sometimes a good idea to help someone else reach an insight;
and the same is true while making the Exercises. Ignatius mentions this in connection with the discernment of spirits. The one
giving the Exercises is to help the exercitant to "unmask the de-
ceptive tactics of the enemy of our human nature" (GU, no. 7). In
part, this is a question of character, but there are not a few persons for whom spiritual insights can occasionally break down
psychic blockages to meditation and prayer. For example, the
insight that there is often some pain underlying anger and depression may help one to come closer to the bedrock of the soul;
or the insight that one has to let the words of Scripture "move
in the heart," as Mary did, can lead to a more free, more existential, and more fruitful dealing with Scripture. To call this
"logotherapy" would be to use too special a word and one too
laden with connotations foreign to the case at hand; and yet, in a
deeper sense, logotherapy is part of the Exercises — a discovery
of meaning and a healing through the Logos of God, who has
become flesh amid human history.

For the One "Who Receives the Exercises"

Up to this point we have been speaking mainly of the one giving
the Exercises, and only indirectly of the one who receives them,
the one "making" them. Obviously a great deal of what has been

said about the one advising the exercitant is also valid for the exercitant: a readiness to internalize and put a good interpretation on what is being given and said; a trustful commitment, and so on. But over and above this, certain observations are meant in a special way for the exercitant and constitute prerequisites for good communication.

1. The exercitants are to give themselves to the Exercises, according to the Book of the Exercises, "with great spirit and generosity" (GU, no. 5). The Spanish reads, *con grande ánimo* and *liberalidad* — with the large, broad soul and the interior freedom that do not wall themselves off from the activity of God's Spirit with their own preconditions.

2. The oft-cited line from Jewish poet Nelly Sachs — "Everything begins with yearning" — fits the basic dynamics of the Exercises exactly. Again and again the exercitant is summoned to take cognizance of the *longing of his heart* and to express to God what he seeks. Yearning is something like a guide beam for the route of the Exercises. Not every wish, not every yearning is fulfilled right away, and not always in the way that we have perhaps hoped for. Nevertheless, longing is the primordial movement leading to God. Augustine has summed it up in exemplary fashion in his Confessions: "Restless is our heart, O Lord, until it rests in you"; and another time he turns it around, even more incomprehensibly: "God's longing is the human being." Encounter, giving, and receiving are all at work in longing.

3. The one making the Exercises must be prepared to "have it out" with the one giving the Exercises as to what is *precisely at issue* for himself. This is clearly shown in the annotation that one should not give everyone the whole four weeks of the Exercises, if the subject would be overtaxed by the nature of the later material or she does not have enough time to devote to it (see GU, 18–19). On the basis of these annotations, the "daily Exercises" have taken shape, suitable for the various situations and opportunities of the exercitants.

4. The exercitant's *will to reach the goal* is an essential attribute of a person who sets off down a road. And so Ignatius

soon proposes the "Principle and Foundation" (see GU, nos. 21, 23). In this text, we have assurance about what is actually at stake on the path of the Exercises and how those involved can feel that they are heading for their goal along this route. Ignatius does not speak of a formal "contract," as people often do nowadays apropos of logo-therapies. But it is important to him that the exercitants at least have an inkling as to what they are becoming involved in. Surprises will be in good supply on the journey; but a certain initial clarity can only be helpful.

5. Ignatius considers the *will to the means* just as essential to the Exercises as the will to reach the goal or end. The seriousness of the will to the end is measured by the seriousness of the will to the means. The means, in the Spiritual Exercises, are the Exercises themselves. "To exercise" is an act of hope. And for the one making the Exercises, the *readiness to "exercise"* is decisive — even when it becomes trying (see GU, no. 12). This readiness is a necessary precondition, although it can be dangerous in a way. It can conceal a will to spiritual achievement that, on the one hand, is important for the exercitant's "starting up," but later can be an enormous obstacle, as if while driving, one kept turning the ignition key. When Ignatius indicates that in times of emptiness and inner malaise the exercitant should lengthen rather than shorten his or her prayer time, this effort is meant to be an expression of the seriousness of one's own search.

6. Of decisive importance is the *daily conversation*. Here openness is important, although one can be patient with oneself: One should be sharing spiritual experiences, not making confessions. It is understandable that there should sometimes be great resistance. But it will often be overcome rather through an understanding, gentle "dealing with oneself" than through acts of coercion.

7. All efforts expended on the Exercises are nourished by a spiritual truth that Meister Eckhart once expressed with the words: "God is more ready to give than the human being to receive." The root of the trust a person can have on a spiritual quest is the infinite self-giving, self-surrender of God.

8. Without *readiness for quiet and listening*, no communication will take place in the Exercises. Meditation weekends today are often held in silence, with "Exercises in complete silence." For Ignatius, this framework and space of silence for the Exercises are something he takes for granted. It is remarkable, however, that he speaks not of silence, but of withdrawal "from all friends and acquaintances, and from all earthly concerns" (GU, no. 20). It is a matter of the "laying aside of cares," of liberation from the network of daily duties, of concentration and attentiveness, of the stilling of the noise that drowns out quiet within the soul.

There is an old joke that might shed some light on the meaning of silence. It goes like this: In outrage, a woman reported to the divorce court that her husband had not spoken a single word to her in ten years. Somewhat incredulous, the judge asked the rather shy husband whether this was true. The husband answered in a low voice, "Yes, Your Honor. I didn't want to interrupt my wife." Some people's experiences with prayer are like that and might explain the complaint that, "God doesn't talk to me when I pray!" God's response might be, "It's so hard to interrupt you when you're presenting all of your requests, cares, and praises"! There is a kind of speaking that is childlike, biblical, as well as adult, and that is described as "pouring your heart out." But there is also such a thing as a spiritual torrent of words that impedes, or even completely prevents, encounter. Ignatius's experience has him say: "The more we keep ourselves alone and secluded, the more fit do we make ourselves to approach and attain to our Creator and Lord, and the nearer we come to him" (GU, no. 29).

Turning away as a prerequisite for turning toward God, for deeper communication — this is what the Exercises are about.

Sophisticated Questioning

Anyone who stands in the living tradition of the Exercises always learns something new. Evidence for the desire to learn and for growing attentiveness can be found in certain questions that are important for the Exercises and show something of their sensitive and sophisticated communication.

1. Possible Questions for the Preliminary Conversation

When Exercises are spread out over a longer period of time, preliminary conversations often take place, or at least there is contact by phone or letter. In that case questions like the following are important:

- What are your hopes and expectations for the Exercises?

- Do you have any fears as you approach the Exercises?

- How many times have you already made the Exercises?

- What was important for you the last time you made them, and how did this eventually work out?

- How is your psychological situation and your ability to handle stress?

- From your experience, what in the Exercises is important, helpful, or dangerous for you?

- What would you like to say about your prayer life?

- Are there any major internal or external decisions coming up?

- What is particularly characteristic of your present life situation?

- Do you have anything else to say that is important to you?

2. By Way of Preparation for Conversation in the Exercises

- What has especially moved me since the last conversation, yesterday?

- What way have I followed, or been led, in my Spiritual Exercises?

- How do I feel?

- Does anything disturb me as I continue the journey?

- What did I feel to be especially helpful?

- Do I feel resistance to anything?

- Do I feel invited to continue in some particular direction?

- What is the goal of my wishing and longing?

- Do I have any questions or complaints regarding the daily conversations?

3. *For Reflection by the One Giving the Exercises*

- What is my general impression or basic feeling regarding the exercitant's way and journey?

- Do I find anything particularly striking?

- Where do I observe movements of the Spirit or the Enemy?

- Where does the exercitant seem invited to further progress, or where does he or she seem "stuck"?

- How did I feel before, during, and after the conversation?

- Did I feel blocked or inwardly free?

- Have I gotten too much into "doing" things?

- What new awareness have I gotten these days about the path of the Exercises?

- What do I experience as important for the service of counseling?

- Do I still have any unfinished business in my mind?

Ignatius would surely say, could he see this list of questions, that we can do a great deal by cooperating with the exercitant, but nothing without experience and the grace of the Lord and his Spirit.

Chapter 5

Communication with Oneself
Prayer of Loving Attention

One of the many humorous and suggestive sayings of comedian Karl Valentin hits the nail on the head when it comes to communication: "Think I'll stop in and see myself tonight. Wonder if I'll be home." Is this not an exact description of what we ourselves experience from time to time? We can be "home," we can be alone, but are we really there with ourselves? We are not "beside ourselves" only when we explode in rage; we can also be beside ourselves, not be with ourselves, when all our attention is directed to the outside. This becomes clearest when we cannot say "how things are going," what our mood is, how we feel, what is going on with us. Not a few sensitivity seminars aim at nothing else than to help persons get in contact with themselves. Even for Ignatius, it was a long journey before he found himself.

Discovery of the World Within

It is not only an edifying story, but actually happens frequently enough, that a store manager, a businessman, or a homemaker busied with many things "comes to himself" or "herself" only during an extended, perhaps life-threatening, illness. Long hours of lying there peacefully, without distraction, without conversation, without reading, can help one to discover one's own inner space and thereby provide an opportunity to communicate with oneself. This was Ignatius's own experience. As he lay in sick bay, he had strange experiences that had far-reaching consequences.

He discovered within himself various motions, sensations, and feelings. The decisive thing was his cognizance of a difference among various effects of his daydreams. When he fantasized an adventure in the service of an elegant lady or great, knightly deeds, he was enthusiastic as long as he reveled in his fantasies. Afterward, however, he experienced rather a stale aftertaste.

It was the other way around when he read Holy Scripture or legends of the saints and fantasized going "barefoot to Jerusalem" to imitate Jesus and the saints. In this case "he was filled with consolation not only while entertaining such thoughts, but he was satisfied and happy after he had turned his mind elsewhere, as well" (BDP, no. 8). The significance of this difference, which he completely missed at first, is clear from his observation: "This was the first consideration that he carried out concerning the things of God. Later, while composing the Book of the Exercises, he began on this basis to gain lucidity concerning the doctrine of the discernment of spirits" (ibid.).

Persons maintaining intimate contact with their world of feelings could regard this event as scarcely worth bringing up. Nevertheless, there are quite a few persons who are not familiar with this access to their own sensations and feelings. It happens over and again that, in a preliminary conversation, persons tell of a massive injustice, for example, but are incapable of speaking about their sensations and feelings. When asked how they feel, the answer often comes in the form of a simple repetition of the story of the injustice suffered, but the vocabulary of annoyance, anger, rage, fear, sorrow, depression, and so on, seems to be missing. Ignatius became acquainted with these inner movements. While one of his brethren was sailing for the new world — America had just been discovered — Ignatius was making the discovery of enormous, mysterious inner worlds.

Compass of the Soul

Where does this path go? How long does it go on? These questions are normal when someone would like to know where a path, an undertaking, a plan lead. They are questions that Ignatius asked too as he made elementary discoveries about his inner stirrings and motions. But he experienced his feelings not just as a series of colorful blobs of paint on the canvas of his soul; he usually saw them as bound up with questions about where he was going in life. What did he want? To pursue a career at court? Or to follow a trail shown him in the saints and in Jesus' disciples? What did God want from him?

Ignatius was concerned in his search with decoding the world of his feelings as well — as indications, signposts, answers. For him, the most significant emotional stirrings were certainly those of joy, of "consolation," and of enthusiasm. When he felt enthusiasm and lasting joy, he moved further, inwardly and outwardly, in this direction. Especially at the sight of the starry canopy of the heavens, he felt in himself consolation, gladness, joy, and a great longing to serve the Lord of the universe (see GU, no. 11). "Inflamed" by this longing, by enthusiasm for ideals, he felt himself moved and driven.

As a simple basic rule, we may say: Whatever brings one lasting feelings of deep joy, peace, freedom, love, and inward relish is a good indication of the right way to follow. Those who follow these impulses — even against many obstacles — can know that they are being borne along the way of life.

False Paths and the Art of Discernment

Granted, it is not always this simple to use the compass of the soul. Ignatius and spiritual tradition often speak of the "temptation in the guise of goodness." Ignatius had this experience especially in a phase of his life during which he was tormented by scruples. He sought in every direction and found no rest for his soul, regardless of how frequently he went to confession. Finally, he was confronted by the temptation to commit suicide. All he had to do was jump through a trapdoor in his cell and plummet to his death. Under the appearance of good — that is, at the invitation to heed ever finer movements of his conscience —

he was being driven by his perfectionism into a spiritual "dead end." This experience resulted in Ignatius's always posing the question: In what direction are my thoughts, ideas, and feelings carrying me? The goal must guide the discernment.

In the presence of similar or almost identical feelings, goals can lead in altogether different directions. There is an inner, "peaceful" mood that is only the sign of a lazy peace, achieved by sealing oneself off from the "evil world without." And there is a peace that lends joy and bestows strength for the challenges of life. The same thing can happen with the feeling of fear. There is a fear that would have one draw back and wall oneself in from confrontations. Conversely, there is a fear that warns of real dangers or leads to getting in touch with someone who can help.

The "discernment of spirits," which was so important to Ignatius, attends to inner feelings and seeks to distinguish in what direction the inner movements would have him go. If they carry him in the direction of more trust, faith, love, and hope, then Ignatius understands this as the direction toward the good. If, by contrast, he notices an inward paralysis, resignation, desperation, then he sees the powers of destruction at work. The first years after his conversion on his sickbed were years in which he cultivated more and more communication with himself, his feelings, and his acts of will.

Gospel of Life

It is almost superfluous to say that Ignatius communicated not only more and more with himself, in a way that could have locked him up in his self. This danger certainly existed for him. But he was too bent on the quest for God, and so communication with himself occurred always as communication with God as well. To put it another way: in his exploration of his life, Ignatius increasingly discovered life itself as a Gospel. The Gospel of Jesus Christ was not only a text read at Mass; it was an event in the midst of life, and in the midst of life he sought and found

God. Ignatius made this discovery in everything that occurred. He reserved a special time every day for expressly connecting his life and God.

For this operation he chose the term "general examination of conscience" (GU, no. 43). Its meaning can be more readily decoded with terms in wider use nowadays: "Daily evaluation," for instance, stresses that we have to uncover the treasures and dangers of a day in our life. The formulation lovingly "feeling through" or "prayer of heed" aims at a loving "feeling through" the events of the day. Just as one can figure out what an object is by feeling it through the packaging, we can try to get a feel for the Spirit of God and his workings through the mask of the day's events.

In the original form of the Examination of Conscience, Ignatius had five steps:

1. In the first step, Ignatius let himself come to an awareness of the fact that he lives in the *presence of God*, whose Name is: I am the I-am-here. In this presence he *thanks God* for all that he has experienced as benefit, as good, as life-bestowing. He will practice this thanksgiving and improve it, and this in the knowledge that ingratitude, as he once put it, is the "source of all evil."

2. In a second step, Ignatius gives rein to his *earnest desire* to attain clarity in his life and be freed from all of the dark, evil, sinful elements that threaten his life and love.

3. In the third step, he reviews the *events of the day*, from morning to evening. He recalls conversations, decisions, encounters, and heads in the direction where he felt in himself inner darkness, movements and stirrings of the Evil Spirit, such as, for instance, false fears, prejudices, fixations.

4. In the fourth step, which organically evolves from the third, he opens himself to the Holy Spirit, to the stream of *reconciliation*, to the phenomenon of liberation, to the satisfaction of his soul.

5. In the last step, Ignatius turns in trust and hope to God's *Spirit of the future*. He gives his inner movement space so that

the power of goodness, of the leaven of the Gospel, of God's loving providence, may permeate his life ever more and more.

Ignatius's five-point list has the sweep of grand words: God and a life of gratitude, truth and freedom, life and the ordering of life, conversion and reconciliation, hope and growth. In the daily practice of this consciousness, a person grows ever more closely bound to God, more truthful, more free, more reconciled, and more hopeful. And this can be summed up by saying the person matures, becoming one who communicates with life more and more and cultivates this communication more and more in the examination of conscience.

Coming to the Point

Alongside the general method of examination, Ignatius uses what he calls a "particular examination" (see GU, nos. 24–31). Here he is like a no-nonsense behavioral therapist, as it were. He asks himself, forthrightly, "What change in my life do I seek?" And he takes this change for his goal and "works on it." Over the weeks, twice a day, he notes on a special piece of paper his assessment of how he has kept his resolution, that is, the behavioral change he has proposed, and observes its development. Such questions and daily projects in his life — what we used to call "good resolutions" — can be: to clean up one's desk in the evening; not to make people with important questions wait forever for an answer; to designate a daily time for prayer; to ask the children at supper about their school day; instead of giving evasive answers, to select a direct, open manner of expression.

This can be about things that pertain more to outward behavior or else such as have to do with deeper consciousness. Many of the examples given may seem petty, and yet the answer given by a wise old man to a starry-eyed young idealist, who asked what he could do for world peace, has something to recommend it: "You could start by closing the door behind you a little more quietly."

A new study — from where else but America — has concluded that those who put their ends and means in writing enjoy far

greater professional success and earn more than persons who
have their plans only in their heads. Obviously there is a particular advantage in writing these things down: the advantage of
clarity. But there may also be the advantage of simply remem-
bering them. An Asian proverb has it: The palest ink is stronger
than the best memory.

All such Exercises can be seen as a creative attempt to improve
communication with our environment. As preparation, it is useful to enter into conversation with ourselves and — essential for
Ignatius — again and again to open ourselves up so that God's
Spirit may be at work in our interior and in our relationships.

From Practice

People often spend many years coming to terms with the education they have gotten from their parents and the world around
them. Not quite so often it happens that, having outgrown
the "foreign education" of their parents and teachers, people
take their education into their own hands. The examination of
conscience, the daily evaluation, the prayer of loving attention
constitute a way of cooperating lovingly and in interior freedom with one's own growth-process. Granted, many obstacles
stand in the way. Let us look at a series of examples intended
to show how, through prayerful daily examination, communication with oneself and one's environment can be improved and
how obstacles that crop up can be dealt with.

1. "Everything's hard at first," or: "How do I acquire a habit,
or get rid of one" could serve as titles for the *difficulty of getting started*. As so often happens in human life, some people are
helped by the "pressure of living": "I've just realized that I can't
take it any more. Life is more something that's happening to me;
I'm not living it. That was the final motivation to take time for
myself every day."

The first question seems indeed to be that of *motivation*.
Why do I want to help myself — for what purpose and with
what means?

2. Alongside the right motivation, the most important thing is the *question of means*. After all, one can say: "Whoever wills the ends, wills the means." The earnestness with which one proposes to reach a goal can be measured by the earnestness with which he or she embraces the appropriate means. If someone wants to climb a peak but doesn't start by going to a practice course or saving up to buy the proper equipment, that person has "peak dreams," it is true, but no "peak will." Now, how can the will to self-help be anchored in one's own life through the prayer of loving attention?

3. The first thing is *choice of the right time and space*. For some people, the first minutes after awakening are exactly right; for others this is the most impossible time. Still others experience the time in the street car or on the train as the ideal moment. Someone else gives herself five or ten minutes in a nearby church, or on a park bench, before going home after work. Or she sets up a little "prayer corner" in her own room. For others, the time before going to sleep at night is best. "A peaceful conscience is the best pillow," the old saying has it. And there is a good deal of truth here.

4. Other help for practice may be found in *imaginative ways of examining one's conscience*. Many married couples find that telling one another how the day has gone is a good way to make such an examination and at the same time helps their relationship to grow. I'm impressed by the custom of one married couple I know: owing to job pressures, breakfast is the only time they have with each other. During this precious half-hour, the pair talk only of themselves and what concerns them. "If something else gets in, we wonder whether everything is okay in our relationship." For someone else, the daily evaluation can take the form of a spiritual smoke. "I open the window, light my cigarette, watch the smoke rise, and with the smoke, my thoughts of the day and its events. This is my burnt-offering to the Lord." Naturally, we must not forget that "The Surgeon General warns, . . ." but it is clear that a pleasant atmosphere can be a great help.

Another says, "I can't afford a therapist, but I can afford God — he does it for free." The context of his remark: "When I'm lying in bed, I just let all thoughts and feelings come, whether they're pleasant or unsavory or scary. God knows me. He knows about me and looks after me lovingly, he knows me. I place my life beneath his gaze." This way of letting a salutary "soul cloud" rise up is similar to a thought expressed in Psalm 139: "O Lord, you have searched me and known me. You know when I sit down and when I rise up; you discern my thoughts from far away. You search out my path and my lying down, and are acquainted with all my ways" (Ps. 139:1–3).

5. This psalm is also appropriate for practicing a simple, *contemplative kind of examination of conscience*. The examination is left to God. True, it makes sense to look at our own life. But may we not also consider the fact that we never see through ourselves entirely, indeed do so only to a very slight extent? Are we not like an island in the ocean, of which only the smallest part projects from the water? And when we go diving near the shore, we generally don't plunge into the uttermost depths. It can be a wonderful, salutary kind of examination of conscience to leave all active examination aside and just be there, sit there, lie there, and leave ourselves to the loving eye of God. "Your servant kneels before your sight, Keep me safe all through the night," was the only evening prayer of a nurse, which was picked up even by the "tough customers" whose sickrooms she visited.

6. For me personally, the prayer of attention in the form of a *"break" prayer* is a good help. I adopted this practice during my years as spiritual director of the German College in Rome. When the new theology students arrived, I always gave them five days of Spiritual Exercises, including a brief conversation with each one each day. That could be fifteen conversations a day, in some years, besides the instruction sessions, celebration of the Eucharist, and so on. After the five days were up, students would sometimes ask me, with a mixture of gratitude, wonder, and interest: "How do you manage to hold up, without becoming totally exhausted?" My somewhat ironic, but absolutely earnestly

meant, reaction consisted in the counter-question: "Have you ever worked for a week with twenty breaks a day?"

Of course, none ever had. Then I could explain that this is what I had done in the past days. After each short conversation I took a minute, or even as many as five minutes, for a "break." I would make a little self-examination. How do I feel now? Am I relaxed or tense? What has especially moved me in the last conversation? Then I would make a long exhalation and commend to God's Spirit the path of the person with whom I had spoken. Then perhaps a good stretch, and a look out the window at the landscape. And then a wait for the next knock to come at my door, and the next student would come to me with a piece of his life mystery.

Little spiritual pauses like that can have an effect like shock absorbers on a car, or the buffers between railroad cars, or the cartilage between vertebrae. If those little elastic protectors are missing, one may feel a terrible grating and unbearable pain. So, why not allow oneself the daily loosening-up exercise of a "break" prayer? Pauses like that can occur on the way from one office to another, or between hanging up the telephone and turning the computer on. The "creative pause" need not always be postponed until one's next vacation. A short, frequent break will often do it as well.

7. For many people, *prayer with the appointments calendar* has become a favorite habit: in the morning, three minutes of looking at the calendar, at the various appointments and the intervals between. What do I see in store for me today? What spurs a positive or negative "reaction" in me? What hopes do I have? Can I believe that God's Spirit works in all things, often enough in a battle with the powers of evil?

The great apostle of love of neighbor Vincent de Paul once told of a morning prayer that a presiding judge confided to him:

Do you know, Monsieur, how I pray my prayer? I glance over what I have to do in the course of the day and draw my conclusions from this as my point of departure: I will

now walk to the Palace of Justice. I have such and such to
do there, and perhaps shall encounter some personage or
other who intends to bribe me. With God's grace I am on
my guard here. Perhaps someone will make me some very
attractive gift — oh, yes, but I don't accept it. And when I
am determined to decide against one of the litigating parties
in a suit, I speak with him calmly and from the heart.

And Vincent asks, after this story: "Now, then, what do you
think of this kind of morning prayer?"

One might well conclude with the question: What are we to
make of this sort of communication with oneself, with one's
own life, and in all this what are we to make of communication
with God?

Chapter 6

Communication and Community

Citizens' initiatives and companies with limited liability, parties and churches, unions and cultural associations, groups and factions, outing clubs and expeditions, leagues and organizations, religious orders and cliques, communes and communities — there is no end to the terms designating various very different forms of groups and communities. That groups and communities involve communication is evident. Without communication, there is no community. Community is communication. It will be worth our while to examine not only Ignatius's communication, but also his community — his idea of community, of the community of a religious order. Each involves the other: community lives on communication, and communication creates community.

"Friends in the Lord": A Composite Picture of a Community

What kind of community did the first companions have with Ignatius? What self-image did they have? The answer to these questions is complex. Here it may help to imagine putting together a kind of "Identi-Kit picture," by analogy with police searches. There the most varied pictures are collected from eyewitnesses. When all of these transparencies are overlaid one on the other, a rough composite picture of the culprit may be created. What are the various "transparencies" or layers in the Ignatian and Jesuit understanding of community, and hence also of communication?

Before we lay the various transparencies one on another, let us consider a self-description that became especially important for the new group around Ignatius. They understood themselves as "friends in the Lord," even though they did not often apply this designation explicitly. They saw themselves as friends of Jesus Christ, as friends of God, and as friends of one another. To formulate it in a different way: *Their belonging to Jesus created their belonging to one another.*

Even when the first period of time was past — like any beginning, it had consisted of a "honeymoon" — the key self-image of this community remained. As a large group, as a religious order, they did not call themselves "friends in the Lord," and Ignatius would never have allowed any formal name but "Society of Jesus." His group was not to be known as "Ignatians." Nor was his community to be defined first and foremost by way of a common pastoral aim. It was to be a community defined by way of a relation: precisely the Society of Jesus.

Granted, the combined layers and transparencies yield only an "Identi-Kit" image. But at times even this leads to "getting their man."

Search-Community of Believers

The first transparency is that of a *search-community* of believing, religious persons. The young men of the new society were all more or less still in search of something. A whole series of them studied at the renowned Sorbonne in Paris. None of them felt that he had reached his goal, either with his life or with his faith. The life of the community fermented like new wine, and their religious search gave them no rest. At this point, Ignatius brought them ahead, as well as together.

A Life-Group of Partners

The second image can be called a *life-group of partners* in the sense that the young men shared or communicated a great deal in their lives together. The later Secretary of the Society of Jesus Juan de Polanco describes the coalescence of the group in the following words:

> The second way to hold these companions together was mutual trust, and manifold mutual communication. As they did not live in the same house, they had the habit of taking their meals sometimes where one lived, sometimes where another lived, depending on mutual inclination, and to assist one another in spiritual as well as temporal things. Thus their mutual affection for one another in Christ grew. These gatherings also helped their studies, and in no small measure. One who had more talent than another in a given area helped the one who had received less. (Wilkens, 228–29).

The intensive group life of this spiritual student community can scarcely be defined more simply and more concretely than to say: they shared what they had.

Common Spiritual Way of Life

The third transparency is that of *common elements of the spiritual life* and a *common spirituality*. One of the first companions once reported that the companions had been surprised to find that, even before they had all come together, they had lived essential elements of their spiritual lifestyle in similar ways. "No wonder," we shall have to say, since they all had gone through the school of Ignatius. For them, spiritual guidance had become important. They had made the Exercises. Prayer, the examination of conscience, and a simple, indeed poor, lifestyle belonged to their life. The sacraments of the Eucharist and Confession had become more and more important to them.

The "Priestly Character": "To Help Persons"

Is the *priestly character*, which attaches to the Jesuit order and which popes sometimes emphasized by way of admonition, important for the question of the art of communication? Yes, in at least one sense: Ignatius understood his priesthood as service to persons, and nothing else. This is most explicit in a formulation taken from the *Pilgrim's Report.* Here Ignatius says of himself: "Since the pilgrim had learned that it was not the will of God that he spend any considerable length of time in Jerusalem, he had constantly considered within himself what he should do now. Finally he came more and more to the conviction that he should study for a while, in order to be able to help souls" (BDP, no. 50).

Ignatius saw something, and he said to himself: If I become a priest, I can speak and preach on spiritual questions with fewer hindrances, I can give persons God's reconciliation in the Sacrament of Reconciliation and celebrate the Eucharist with them. So I shall study and become a priest! Ignatius does not speak of special inner experiences and illuminations, as he does in so many other connections. He becomes a priest because, on a simple rational level, he thinks that this is the way to serve persons' salvation better. It is typical that Father Nadal once began a talk to his confreres with the apology: "I must mention, by the way, that I forgot yesterday to tell you that Father Ignatius was ordained a priest" (O'Malley, 187). Not one single time in the voluminous statutes of his order does Ignatius mention priestly ordination. As dry and rational as all this may sound, none of it "hindered" Ignatius from being mystically touched, most inwardly, in every Mass that he celebrated.

Nor does the priesthood appear among the companions of Ignatius in anything but a matter-of-fact hue. Many are already priests, or on the way to the priesthood, when they join Ignatius. They take it for granted that this is the way for them to serve men and women in the discipleship of Jesus and in the church. They speak more about their calling to the Society of Jesus than to the priesthood. Some young Jesuits wish to be ordained only if the superior orders them to be, as they fear that the priesthood means the danger of a place of honor.

Looked at in this way, the "priesthood as a special theme"

may have much to do with communication, or with today's difficulties of communication in the church. An Ignatian under-standing of priesthood could perhaps help to defuse one of the worst crises in the church, the sometimes almost destructive tension between lay people and priests. A practice of service, actually lived by all Christians, would have to discover not only a "cooperative pastoral practice," but a corresponding theology of the various services and their unity.

Community of Service and Mission

The Society of Jesus has always understood itself as a *commu-nity of mission*, as a *missionary community*. According to the testimonial of Juan de Polanco, "the hope of preaching among the infidels or of dying for Christ decisively contributed to the unity of the community. Common goals are constitutive for any community. "Work in the Lord's vineyard" is a stock expression, and it describes the common goal. That the work is carried on in different places, and that one plows, another prunes, and a third harvests, is of secondary importance. The nature of their community lies especially in the fact that all are in the service of the same Lord and God. This picture also makes it plain that an essential meaning of obedience does not consist in gathering a "powerful army"; Ignatius had always found obedience to be a bond of unity, and it is unity rather than might that inspires him.

In the early years of the order Jesuits said, "Our house is the world." That had a special implication for the way the Jesuits thought of themselves as an apostolic community. "House" did not refer primarily to the Jesuits' places of residence; it refers pri-marily to the interior flexibility and mobility of the community: our house is not a monastery, it is not a residence in the sense of a permanent dwelling place; rather the community house is to be likened to a house-trailer. Our house is the place where the service rendered is evaluated, where, in common spiritual decision-making, new assignments and new missionary tasks are sought. The structural danger, of course, is that such a house could become the place of common absence. But the characteristic feature remains. The point is to be mobile and to live the faith, to witness and proclaim.

Pastoral-Style Community: Our Manner of Proceeding

The more the companions bonded together and the more they gave themselves to the care of souls, the more they became a *pastoral-style community*. It is very significant that the companions spoke of *noster modus procedendi*, "our manner of proceeding." This means that they had the consciousness of a style of their own, through which they were clearly enough distinguished from others. Elements of this style are:

1. No common recitation of the Divine Office, in order to be as mobile as possible.

2. Launching projects, and then, if necessary, leaving it to others to carry them on.

3. Care of souls among youth, among the poor, among simple persons, and likewise among the wealthy and powerful.

4. The "most urgent needs" and caring for those in no one's care, take priority in the services offered.

5. A care of souls inspired by the spirituality of the Exercises, and by the Exercises themselves, in which Jesuits understood themselves as — according to Father Nadal — "servants of consolation."

6. Encouragement of spiritual conversation in groups.

7. Special methods for spiritual decision-making, as, for example, what today is often named *deliberatio communitaria*, a joint or common decision-reaching.

8. Procedural methods orientated to reality and subject to the question of what will help more under what circumstances and what personal constellations.

9. In preaching and catechesis, "service to the word" always playing an essential role.

In the question of a "particular style," the *importance of spiritual conversation* must be especially mentioned, since it is not widely known. Father Nadal transmits to us his interpretation to the effect that "pious conversations" were the origin of the Society of Jesus (see O'Malley, 135). This kind of conversation was important at first for the Jesuits' internal structure, but then it had a strong impact on their pastoral theory and practice. They promoted the creation of spiritual conversation circles where the presence of a priest wasn't always needed to moderate or lead the conversation. It could be the sacristan or whoever had a good feeling for a group and for questions of faith.

When one thinks of all the fears and resistance that flared up in the last few decades in response to the burgeoning spiritual conversation groups, one may wonder what was the standard around the beginning of the community's formation and of Jesuit pastoral practice.

Community of Communication: An Ongoing Miracle

For a complete picture of the community, a transparency labeled "communication community" must be added on, representing a peculiar feature of Ignatian community. In connection with the Jesuits' most recent General Congregations, the topic of apostolic communities often came up. This term is freighted with great tension. An apostolic community, literally translated, is a "gathering" of persons who have been sent out, so to speak, a "convention" of persons sent out! To live this way of life in a balanced way is an art, indeed a miracle. That is the drift of a letter that the superior general of the Jesuits, Peter-Hans Kolvenbach, wrote to the Jesuits. "In their involvement with society the world over, the General Congregation was conscious of the fact that the community — that unit of persons who picked out one another for a lifelong collaboration — constitutes an ongoing miracle."

And this miracle ever demands a lifelong effort in "the art of communication."

Ecclesial Community: Feeling with and in the Church

In its particularity as a mission community, the Ignatian-Jesuit community also sees itself essentially and expressly as an *ecclesial community*, and this in a number of ways. It understood itself as a community of disciples, and a church is essentially a community of the disciples of Jesus. As confirmed by the church, the Jesuits' community of disciples exists because it has been recognized as a religious order. It also owes more to the favor of the popes than might be supposed from its temporary suppression (1773–1814) by Clement XIV. Conversely, thanks to its peculiar features, the order has also given much to the church. The Jesuits were often called *preti riformati,* "reform priests." So we see a balancing act between a critical will to tear down and "reform" and a "dynamic fidelity" to the church community.

The notorious eighteen "Rules for Thinking with the Church, in order to have the true feeling in the Church Militant" (GU, nos. 352–70) would need their own, detailed interpretation. Here the "abyss of history" is of great importance, dividing us from Ignatius by entire centuries. Perhaps one can concisely summarize the message of the Rules, which after all are rules of communication — in three key sentences:

1. Ecclesial community lives by the confidence that the same Spirit of God works in creation, in the commandments, in the church, and in the heart of the individual — and continues to do so today, through conflict and consensus, binding these fields of activity together.

2. Ecclesial community lives only if its members feel deep within them a gratitude for this community and bring this gratitude to concrete expression.

3. Ecclesial community lives only if a necessary critique of persons is forthcoming in a manner calculated to be effective.

Even if the images mentioned provide only a rough sketch for our composite picture of community, we can sense just how complex community is. Experiences and rules, sympathy and antipathy, constantly shifting situations and solid goals demand to be lived, and lived to the hilt. Community is a work of art, community is a "miracle." All this only shows how important it is to foster communication.

Constitutions of the Order: "The Law of Love"

Although Latin has long ceased to be the language of Jesuit instruction, a number of Latin "linguistic fossils" still pop up when Jesuits are speaking colloquial German. Most of these peculiar usages are concerned with especially important statements. One of these important "word relics" is the phrase *interna lex caritatis* — the "inner law of love." The combination of words, "law of love," strikes one at once as rather odd, like, for example, the Pauline formulation, the "perfect law of freedom." But the place where this turn of phrase originates is just as important and eloquent as its internal make-up is paradoxical: the "inner law of love" is spoken of in the foreword to the Constitutions, with their nearly seven hundred paragraphs and divisions. This preamble expresses two fundamental convictions.

The first states that the "highest wisdom and goodness of God preserves, leads, and guides the Society of Jesus." And the second, "that on our side, more than any exterior statutes, the inner law of love and goodness, which the Holy Spirit writes and engraves on hearts, contributes to the way and growth of the communities" (SGJ, no. 134). As a plus or a minus before an entry on a balance sheet shows whether the entry is a debit or credit, so the phrase the "inner law of love" stands as the key-signature for all the ensuing statutes. The articles aim to give support for a way of life based on the Gospel, the Good News. All laws and rules aim to be the expression of, and help for, the life of a large spiritual community.

Ignatius knew about anxiety and scrupulosity from his own life. Hence he determined that the articles of the Constitutions should not bind "under sin." These statutes serve to describe a way of discipleship in community, a way to the handing on of the Gospel. They breathe the spirit of community, the spirit of the care of souls, the spirit of the imitation of Christ. Admittedly, over the centuries, and especially in the last General Congregation, these statutes have been adapted, updated, and supplemented again and again. True, they breathe the spirit of their time, but words like the "inner law of love" are abidingly valid: they shape the inner dynamics and vitality of the Constitutions and are not merely a pious preamble, after which we get down to business, that is, to legislating love, paragraph by paragraph. The Constitutions are ultimately concerned with a living community, and hence with communication, as we see in an expression that one lately hears Jesuits using a great deal: "From the *I* of the Exercises to the *we* of the Constitutions." This means that the Exercises are in a way focused more on the individual, his conversion, his calling, while the Constitutions do the same for the collective self-understanding, the corporate identity, the "we" of community.

Dealings between Superior and Subject

The position of communication in a community becomes especially clear when we consider how it understands the roles its members play, when we look at various positions and assignments. A letter dated December 1, 1554, addressed to the Italian members of the Society, and May 29, 1555, to the Jesuits in Spain, can be regarded as the key text for conversation between two Jesuits, of whom the one is a superior, the other a subject. The items published in this letter represent extracts from the Constitutions of the order and are therefore of great importance, so that they ought to be set forth in detail. They are also capable of "straightening out" the cliché of "blind obedience."

1. Let him who would submit a matter to a superior first consider it carefully within himself, and discuss it with others, to the extent it has importance. Whether in minor or urgent matters, when time does not allow for a longer discussion or private consideration, naturally it will be left to each one's prudence and good sense whether he should submit the matter to the superior without this preparation.

2. Once reflected upon and considered, these questions should be presented in more or less the following words: "I have thought about such and such (or spoken about it with others) and we (or I) wondered whether such and such might be a good idea." But never tell the superior in dealing with him, "This or that is good." Express it conditionally; for instance: "If this or that is the case...."

3. After this discussion, it is up to the superior either to decide the matter at once, to take time for reflection, or to refer the matter to one or more persons who have already considered it, or to assign someone else to look into and assess the matter, depending on its urgency or difficulty.

4. When someone has an objection to the superior's decision or suggestion as to the right way to proceed, and the superior continues to hold his opinion, then, for the time being, there are no grounds for objection or disagreement.

5. But if, after this decision on the part of the superior, one is nevertheless of the conviction that something else would be better, or if a person believes he has some grounds for a view of which he is not entirely certain, after three or four hours, or on the following day, he may again present to the superior the question whether this or that would be good; but one must always use a tone and manner of expression so that no inner conflict or ill humor is either present or

noticeable. For this reason it would be best to pass over
the previous decision in silence.

6. Even with the matter once or twice discussed and at length
   decided, one may, after a month or more, again bring up
   what one feels and thinks, once more in the way that we
   have given. For experience affords, with time, a better ac-
   quaintance of many things, some of which also change in
   the course of time.

7. Nevertheless, the petitioner is to be governed by the character and prevailing frame of mind of the superior and speak
   explicitly, clearly, and in an audible voice, and where possible, come at times that are convenient for the superior.
   (TW, 183–84)

Like the letter on communication to the confreres at the Council of Trent, this, too, is a letter in which almost every sentence
could practically melt in your mouth. What a culture of conversation in an order that was especially famous, or infamous, for
"blind obedience!" Does every supervisor and every employee of
a modern business enterprise, as we enter the third millennium,
have this kind of conversational culture as his or her model and
example? It's not even clear whom Ignatius was more intent on
hammering his message into, superiors or subordinates. Presumably both. What encouragement he offered to the cultivation
of conversation! This becomes still clearer if we summarize the
letter in the form of rules for conversation:

1. Don't come crashing in with all kinds of ideas. Go over
   them thoroughly in your mind.

2. As far as possible, consult with others. You too need their
   experience and advice.

3. Don't speak apodictically and in a tone of infallibility. Give
   the other person's opinion a chance too.

4. First bring up all reasons, arguments, and responses, even
   when there are obstacles to them.

5. After the phase of argumentation, leave the decision to those whom it concerns.

6. As superior, examine which way the matter can be well thought through and scrutinized, before it is decided.

7. Present your opinion repeatedly, even when a decision has been made by the superior.

8. Trust time and growing experience. Your request may become clearer. Superiors may learn something new, and you may apply again, after weeks or months.

9. Adjust to the manner and particularity of your superior. Each one needs to be dwelt with differently. In so doing you increase the chances that your petition will be better received.

10. Present your requests explicitly, clearly, understandably, and at a favorable moment.

In his controversial book *Die Kleriker* (The clerics), Eugen Drewermann cites physicist and Nobel laureate Albert Einstein to the effect that, for brainless, military obedience, no cerebrum is necessary; just a brain stem would suffice. Drewermann thinks that this is an accurate picture of Ignatian obedience.

How would Ignatius have conversed with the two? Perhaps he would have surprised them.

Profile of the Governance of the Superior General: Goodness, Love, Good Judgment, and Knowledge

It would take a whole volume to present the significance and expressiveness of the Constitutions for communication. But here we can concentrate on the decisive perspectives of communication in "personalized form," the form that Ignatius describes when he speaks of "how the superior general should be." This description shows the ideal image of encounter and leadership

that Ignatius has in mind. Here we have a clear look at an unusual image of a strong person capable of making judgments, a
loving leadership-personality, who has knowledge of the world
in a high measure and is deeply bound to God. It also shows
that not only good structures are important, but, even more,
individuals with charisma, wisdom, and ability.

- The superior general shall be entirely bound to God as
  the "source of all good," which thus leaves its mark on
  everything that flows from it (SGJ, no. 723).

- "In particular," he must have "love for all neighbors . . . and
  true humility, which will make him most deserving of love
  on the part of God our Lord and human beings" (ibid.,
  no. 725).

- "He must also be free of all passions, . . . lest they disturb
  his rational judgment" (ibid.).

- He must have "such outward serenity and, especially, such
  balance in his speech, that no one can notice any unedifying
  word or other thing about him" (ibid., no. 726).

- "At the same time, he should know how to combine the
  necessary straightforwardness and authority with kindness
  and mildness, so that he neither allows himself to be dissuaded from the decision that he judges more pleasing to
  God our Lord, nor ceases to have appropriate sympathy
  for his sons" (ibid., no. 727).

- "Magnanimity and boldness of heart" are necessary for
  him, in order not "to lose courage in the face of obstacles,
  even if they come from great and mighty persons" (ibid.,
  no. 728).

- "One who will be responsible for so many learned persons" — Ignatius already sees this coming — must be
  endowed with great understanding and judgment. But even
  more necessary are "the prudence and the experience in

spiritual and inner things that will enable him to discern the various spirits" (ibid., no. 729).

- In order to be able to carry matters through to their conclusion, he must have initiative, care, and perseverance (ibid., no. 730).

- He shall not be too old, on the one hand, since the exertions of his task will then tend to surpass his strength. On the other, he shall of course not be too young, since "ordinarily...the authority and experience" would then be lacking that he needs for his office (ibid., 729).

- For dealing with persons and matters outside the Society, the main requirements will be "trustworthiness and a good reputation" (ibid., no. 733).

We shall report the conclusion of the list verbatim. It might make any superior sweat:

- In particular, he should be of the number of those who have most distinguished themselves in virtue, and he should have very great merit in the Society and be very long known as having such. And if he should be lacking any of the above mentioned qualities, he should at least not be deficient in great kindness as well as love for the Society, and good judgment accompanied by good knowledge, should not fail him. For the rest, the helps that he will have,...with God's help and favor can make up for many things (ibid., no. 735).

Tools of the "We"

It is not the primary purpose of this book to present a management model, or one of Jesuit organization. The primary object is communication in the "normal" sense. Still, some passing mention should be made of some aids, stylistic methods, and "instruments of the we" that were significant for Ignatius.

1. Often enough, Ignatius gave his companions precise *descriptions of their goal, for the sake of their path to it.* These also explained the method, the way to the goal. An entire series of such instructions has survived and elucidates how much the clarity of the goal helps for the path. Hardly ever do these descriptions fail to point out that, of course, one must make a more precise observation "on the spot" and make decisions in the light of concrete circumstances.

2. For himself, for his own decisions, Ignatius relied on *expert reports.* A whole series of such reports contains ten, twenty, and more, viewpoints, facts, and rules that were decisive for dealing concretely with a question.

3. *Consultations* with his advisory board belonged to the daily routine. Often he met with his counselors twice on the same day. On these occasions he stuck closely to the agenda. As a sign that there was only one issue, and that they should stick to it, he would place an orange on the table. Undisciplined changing the subject was not allowed. Nor did he himself change the subject "without seeking permission" from those present (MEVI, no. 169). He held himself to the same standards that he demanded of others. The main thing he did was listen attentively to each member of the council. "All the fathers of the consulting body brought paper, on which they indicated what our Father wished them to do about the matter. He then questioned each one in order and never dealt with more than one issue. And so he listened to and responded to all, until time was up. And at the end of the hour, he rose and ended the consultation" (ibid.). With this style of consultation we shouldn't overlook the fact that normally no specific decisions were made. The point was to gather the opinions and experiences of each individual; one matter was concentrated on, and as a rule only one matter was handled.

4. It will be worth our while, to conclude this section, briefly to present the procedure of *delegation* within a community. Father da Câmara writes that Ignatius wished "the provincials to have all possible freedom in running their provinces, and

that they in turn not prejudice the authority of the rectors and other local superiors vis-à-vis their respective subjects" (MEVI, no. 270). In a letter to a provincial, Ignatius wrote:

> Nor is it the office of the provincial, or of the general, to become involved in particular cases. Even if he possessed every possible skill in their regard, it is better that he appoint others to take care of them.... I use this method myself, and I get from it not only help and relief, but also more peace and certitude in my soul. Therefore, as your office demands, have love, and undertake your reflection with the universal good of your province in mind. And as for the good order that ought to obtain in all of these various matters, listen to those who, in your judgment, have the best sense of them. (Ibid.)

As the basis for this conception of leadership, da Câmara cites the following considerations. In the first place, it is simply impossible for the superior general to attend "to a thousand individual matters" (MEVI, no. 271). "And if he does attend to them, how is it possible for him to have knowledge of the many particularities involved, on which the resolution of the matter ordinarily depends? How can the provincial be led by laws and general rules where things are such that every day so many and such different circumstances obtain, completely changing the state of affairs?" (ibid.).

Knowledge and power, which are necessary for all good leadership, should be bound together as closely as possible — otherwise the paradoxical situation will occur that the one who has little knowledge of the concrete situation makes the decision, and the one "who has the knowledge, and has his hand right in the matters, has no power to execute them himself" (MEVI, no. 272). The dilemma of governance that divides knowledge and power could not be sketched more concretely.

Further, the danger exists that someone with all power in hand will lead a subordinate authority to meddle in other people's areas of responsibility, because it has been assigned none of its own: "For if one limits the provincial and takes what is due his office, the provincial seizes upon the domain of the rector, and the rector, for the same reason, upon that of the minister, and so forth, and thus the order of governance, which the Holy Spirit gave to our blessed Father, will be greatly disturbed" (ibid.).

Finally, yet another interesting theological reason may be cited for keeping knowledge and power close. The conception of leadership that delegates both knowledge and power, in very close mutual connection,

> is also based on the fact that God our Lord especially assists the immediate, lower superior in the special things that properly and immediately belong to his office. To reduce the number of these things, or to wish to govern with universal rules, means to deprive him of his office of superior, and consequently to hinder the contribution of that special grace of God that, since it relates to an individual agent, has more effectiveness for such affairs than any other has. (MEVI, no. 271)

To reduce the complex theological proposition to a brief statement: Let God work where God seeks to work — in the concrete sphere, in the persons that God has endowed with value and creativity. The Devil isn't the only one in the details; God's Spirit also works altogether concretely, on the scene and in each of God's creatures.

Conflicts and Resolutions

That Ignatius was a master of communication does not mean that he didn't have problems in dealing with persons. On one occasion he fell under suspicion of heresy; he was involved in legal proceedings; he had confrontations especially with Nicholas Bobadilla, the *enfant terrible* of the first companions; at the thought of a certain candidate for the papacy, his bones shook; and he almost had to dismiss Simon Rodriguez, one of the first companions, from the order.

What he could bring to the art of communication, and to communication "tricks," that he did. Many such steps and options appear in the chapter on "Helps to Communication." On occasion, however, Ignatius resorted to "ex-communication" — to the dismissal of a confrere. At times he did so very abruptly, by today's standards, contrary to his usual habit of waiting with long and loving patience. But obviously Ignatius had also experienced the fact that there are situations and persons with whom only a snip-snap discharge will do. Even in a community, there can be "infections" and blockades that can lead to a crippling of community life. That helps no one.

An example of such a situation, recalls Father da Câmara, was

A German, a student of the Society in Vienna in Austria, who fell into such a delusion that he said that our Lord had given him the spirit of Saint Paul. And although in everything else he was understanding and clever, the Devil brought him, through this evil principle alone, to all manner of disobedience. He said that the authority the Society had, which he would have to obey, derived from the pope as the successor of Saint Peter. And now Saint Paul, whose spirit he had, was not less than Saint Peter, so that he was not obliged to obey the Society. This person ended his course in Vienna in all peace and calm, without notifying anyone of anything, and when it was ended came with this. . . . No grounds or arguments that we proposed to him sufficed, as he gave to everything, in all certitude and composure, the same answer; and in all other matters he spoke and argued very well. As our Father saw this, he dismissed him at once, on the basis of a unanimous decision. (MEVI, no. 283)

Precisely when it comes to painful critical points like reception into a community and dismissal from it, we see the need for communication in a special way. As principles for this, we may cite: being open, without monopolizing; delimiting, without excluding; making one's presence felt and maintaining identity, without building a position for oneself.

Ignatius, who had sometimes striven with all his might to keep a Jesuit in the order, later, toward the end of his life, said that if he had to do it all over again, he would have been much more strict about letting people in.

Chapter 7

Communication and Organization

It makes a great difference for communication whether two persons are taking a silent walk in the woods together, or business partners are negotiating a contract, or someone is defending his or her political views on television. And there is a great difference between whether Ignatius seeks to enter into conversation with himself, or opens himself to God in prayer, or carefully listens to someone's life secret in giving the Exercises, or comes on the scene as architect of a large order, which at his death numbered about a thousand members. The following section will offer some sketches of the organization and architectonics of his community.

The Secretariat

A religious community with hundreds of members, in touch with thousands of persons, does not live only by the charisma of a single person. It needs a little group who have their eye on the big picture, who maintain connections intact, and who keep the flow of information going. This is a fair description of the first Jesuit Secretariat in Rome, today standing just opposite the Vatican. It is not the task of this book to describe the Secretariat and its work of communication in detail. It will be worthwhile, however, to glance briefly at this Ignatian-Jesuit communications office.

A not very well-known document from the year 1547 offers us a report "on the Office of the Secretary, who will be in Rome." This text, with its ninety-one sections, is at the same time a little *handbook for administration, a guide for communication, and an outlook on the spirituality of the daily life of the Office.* The composition is a first result, and an example, of the close collaboration between Ignatius and his secretary, Juan de Polanco, who held the office of Secretary of the Society of Jesus until the year of his death in 1573.

The Medium of Writing

The "Secretary's purpose," writes Ignatius in this paper (probably composed in large part by Polanco himself), "is the same as that of the superior" (GGJ, 830). The fitting means is "writing." Writing has two functions: it is intended to bridge the distance in space between the center of institutional administration and the absent members, and at the same time the distance in time for which memory, being weak, is often insufficient. Writing serves as an aid for the problems of communication that arise from space and time. This little piece of office philosophy brings Ignatius, in his foreword, straight into connection with the Giver of all good gifts: "For God has endowed us with this help, since our spoken language cannot span the distance separating us from those to whom there is something to be communicated, nor can memory be fully sufficient with respect to so many things that demand recall" (ibid.). Letters, couriers, and archives make possible memory, contacts, nearness, communication, and encounters that otherwise would not be possible, or at least not in that way. (Of course, there is no question but that today Ignatius would use the most modern and best means of office and business communication — after, of course, a careful cost-benefit calculation.)

The Goal: One's Neighbor and Humane Encounter — to the Glory of God

The main goal for the Secretary and his collaborators is: "Profit to one's neighbors and strengthening, unity, and consolation for the members of the Society" (ibid.). The whole operation has to pulsate with this goal-seeking, if it is not to turn into a soulless mechanism.

After this grand statement of the goal, there's a special interest in remarks that show Ignatius calling attention to the fact that one has to do with different persons, and that their manner is always to be taken account of. It is worthwhile to deal with what Ignatius can say on less than a page about nuanced relations with different human beings.

In a section on letter writing, nearly every sentence is a gem. When the Secretary writes to individuals:

> In order to write prudently, he should take care to know the person to whom he is writing and pay attention to his particularities, in order to adapt to him as far as possible, whether he is from outside the Society or belongs to it. If he is from outside, prudence demands that one write with more reverence to persons who are great in affairs of the world; to difficult and rough persons, with more mildness and more restraint; to the simple and jovial, more openly; to the witty or brilliant, with more care; to the learned, in a more scholarly tone; to the sorrowing, in a spirit of sympathy; to sure friends, with more trust; to persons not so sure, more cautiously, and in this case one must write short letters to test their willingness, showing them love, and so on; to persons not well known, with reverence and obligingly, without lowering oneself overmuch; to those without high standing, with much friendliness, not condescendingly, but as on an equal or lower level, and so on. And it is to be noticed that, ordinarily, more circumspection is necessary with first letters, especially to unknown persons. And let one take care to reveal the pious motive that has moved one to write to them. (GGJ, 836)

Any secretary, and any lover of pious exclamations or litanies, after reading such a compact analysis of various persons, can only cry, "Saint Ignatius, pray for us!" What attention to one's correspondents! What a keen sense of differences; what a sure instinct for dealing with people!

Office work must be defined from the perspective of its ultimate goal. One must visualize that, despite the predominantly indirect manner of encounter, one *is* meeting real people. And Ignatius sees office work in the perspective of the whole meaning of life: when the secretary is either setting to work, or working on especially important matters, "let him take pains to raise his mind to God, offering to the divine glory and honor what he wishes to do" (GGJ, 848).

Organized to the Very "Sand Sprinkler"

Of course office work starts all over again every morning: organizing records, taking care of materials, the mail, minutes, and so on. And so the document also contains a whole series of altogether concrete instructions: tearing up letters that are no longer needed, inserting the date of dispatch or receipt in the case of important letters; excerpting the essential points for superiors; keeping them all in good order; noting points for a reply; retaining what "comes through about the person writing"; making copies and filing important material in the archives. Let the style of writing be "clear, but not studied or making a great show of one's care"; "let the handwriting be good, or at least readable, clear, and correct"; "seal the letters and send them promptly, affixing postage when necessary"; and one should "be friends with some persons who will deliver the letters" (GGJ, 829–51).

Once again a brief quotation can show how communication is grounded to the last concrete detail, and at the same time afford a glance into a sixteenth-century secretariat:

> It is necessary that [the Secretary] have the mechanical instruments ready, such as well-cut pens, paper, ink, thread, wax, knife, scissors, seal, sand sprinkler; and it would be well to have a writing room to keep papers one is working on, and some bags for writings or letters that are not

needed at the moment; and a box in which to keep official documents, and other things of importance, where they will be ordered according to their titles; for such order is very necessary in this office. (GGJ, 848).

Culture of Letter Writing in the Service of the Apostolate, Unity, and the Work of Publicity

A brief glance into the writing room of the Secretariat of the young Society of Jesus has already shown us some things concerning the composition of letters. But the culture of letter writing is of such great importance for Ignatius that some matters have to be spelled out here. First there is the fact that over six thousand letters of Ignatius are extant, the largest corpus of letters of his time. Many were composed by himself, but many were prepared by his Secretary and edited and signed by Ignatius.

The first kind of letters are *personal letters*, which frequently serve as a written vehicle of spiritual counsel. They are also a testimonial to his loyalty, since some of them are addressed in part to persons who have appeared at the beginning of his spiritual journey. Hugo Rahner has published a whole volume of letters to women. Most of Ignatius's personal letters are responses, that is, Ignatius is reacting to inquiries, needs, or concerns and writes not simply to maintain a correspondence or to "chat." The letterhead — an autograph small cross and the name of Jesus — reproduces the spiritual atmosphere of the entire document. The letter will often begin with an expression like "the most exalted grace and love of Christ our Lord be ever to our constant favor and help" (BU, 80). Hundreds, if not thousands, of these letters end with an expression like, "I close by asking God our Lord to deign, for the sake of his infinite and exalted goodness, to give us his grace in plenitude, that we may experience his most holy will and fulfill it completely" (BU, 81).

Of course, these more personal letters of Ignatius could well be evaluated for the practice of communication exemplified in them, for their style, and so on. But since we are concerned with communication and organization, it will be more to the point to speak of what motivates Ignatius, particularly in connection with his official letter writing. A whole series of important, wide-ranging letters and instructions addressed to the entire order deal exclusively with this topic. This official letter-writing culture had three main concerns. The first was to ensure the unity of the young, rapidly growing community, scattered throughout the world. The second was to be able to provide a coordinated campaign of pastoral work through the flow of information. And third, the question of the public and of public opinion was extremely important.

In 1547, the first year of his tenure as Secretary of the order, Juan de Polanco introduces himself to the order and, at Ignatius's request, of course, takes up the theme of letter writing in his first document. Writing, he says, is the principal medium of mutual contact and is of the highest importance. In an appeal reminiscent of Jesus' saying, "The children of this world are more resourceful than the children of light," he seeks to motivate his confreres to frequent writing:

> And it certainly seems to me that merchants and the other business people of the world very much shame us in this respect. Concerning their miserable little interests they write one another letters and keep their books with an attention and order calculated to enable them to attend better to their trivialities. And we, in the spiritual matters whose interest consists in our neighbor's eternal salvation and in the glory and honor of God, should, even if reluctantly, take a little care and order in writing, which we know would be so very helpful to us. (BU, 161)

After this general and basic attempt at motivation, Polanco adduces an entire battery of reasons for the importance of communication by letter — *twenty* numbered reasons and motives: the unity of the congregation, the strength resulting from unity, reciprocal love and encouragement and correction, the reputation and growth of the order, the reinforcement of gratitude for the great good reported.

"The twentieth and last reason is that thereby God's glory and praise grows — the goal of the entire universe" (BU, no. 164). Now, then, who would still be unwilling to write informative, orderly, and edifying letters?

In the instruction included in this letter of Polanco's on letter writing we also see an abundance of viewpoints that testify to the realism, concreteness, and sensitivity that communication by letter must have in order to be effective. The letters must answer the following questions: Who is the person writing the letter and what are his responsibilities? What is the anticipated fruit of the work? What help is available from influential people? What opposition is there? What sort of popular reputation does he have? What are the spiritual services being rendered? What secular and ecclesiastical events are of interest? Who is entering the community, and what is there to be said of those entering in respect of "bodily appearance, age, health, class, possessions, language, talent, doctrine, spirit?" (BU, 170). How is his health? How is his manner of life? And to include everything, Polanco concludes, "and in general all that a friend would wish to know about another friend" (BU, 171). This remark is important and precious. It recalls the self-image of the first Jesuits as "friends in the Lord." Without this basis, one could regard all of the guidelines cited as simple control mechanisms of an effectively organized business operation.

In the Style of a Wife

For the Ignatian style, which seeks to put more into "love . . . than into words" (GU, no. 230), as we read in the Book of the Exercises, it is characteristic to be more concerned with the matter at hand than with an extravagant style. An entire series of reminders points in this direction. For instance, Polanco once wrote a letter, at Ignatius's direction, to a certain Robert Claysson, of Bruges, with whom a stilted, flowery, long-winded style in both the spoken and the written word had become habitual:

Eloquence and beauty of speech are one thing in profane
speech, and another in religious. As with a wife a demure
adornment is to be recommended, expressive of modesty,
so we approve, in the manner of speech of which ours
make use in speaking or writing, not so much a style for
style's sake, an extravagant youthful eloquence, but rather
an earnest, mature one, especially in letters, whose style
by its very nature should be more terse and polished, and
should be rich in an abundance of things rather than in
words. (BU, 720)

At any rate Secretary Polanco concedes to the wife a certain
"adornment" and to letters too. But the main point is that it
is not so much the words, the garnish, that should be attended
to, but the good, nutritious roast itself. With kindness, but very
clearly, Polanco adds: "May your love take in good part what
our love thinks it ought not to disguise: for we dare not send your
letters anywhere without heavy editing" (ibid.). That is juicy,
plain cooking, garnished a little with love! An even more bitter
mouthful is administered to another wordy writer:

Good progress is demonstrated not through elegant words,
but through deeds. And the time used up in seeking a fancy
vocabulary would be better devoted to other, more fruitful
things. And so you are expressly ordered: the letters that
you have to write every week . . . should be not over two
sentences long. (BU, 917)

One wonders whether the good father felt particularly re-
stricted! With two appropriately constructed sentences it is
possible to fill a whole page!

For the Public: The "Edifying Main Letter"

The Jesuits' periodic letters to Rome are either "main letters"
or "accessory letters." This distinction had been explained in
detail as far back as 1542 in a letter to Peter Faber. The main

letter should be able to be shown publicly, to the community of the order as well as to the larger public. This means that it should be crisply written and well thought out. To make the point concretely, Ignatius wrote to Peter Faber:

> Just the other day it happened to me that it was necessary, or very advisable, to show letters from two of the Society to two cardinals, who were to take charge of things relating to what they had written. And since in these letters there were things that did not belong to the matter, and were without order, and not to be shown, I found myself very hard put to show them parts of the letters and to conceal parts. (BU, 82)

The annoyance is understandable. Playing hide-and-seek did not suit Ignatius — having to use the sleeve of his cassock to cover up or expose various paragraphs in the letters. Ignatius was himself willing, on occasion, to draft a letter several times. "For what one writes, one must observe much more than what one says. For writing abides, and continues to give testimony, and is not so available to improvement or explanation as when we speak" (BU, 83).

The main letter should be "showable." It serves the work of publicity. Hence it must be "edifying." This word sounds too "edifying" today; actually it signifies nothing but "constructive." Letters should serve the apostolate, the unity of the Jesuits, and their "image" among the public. For centuries Jesuit missionaries were among the pioneering discoverers of peoples and lands. Their reports were not infrequently both sensations from little known regions of the world and at the same time glowing missionary reports. The letters of Far East missioner Francis Xavier, especially, had a powerful effect throughout Europe.

The Accessory Letter: "The Jesuits' Little Daughters"

The situation with the accessory letter looked a little different from the one with the "constructive main letters":

I leave for the accessory letters the remaining details that do not belong to the matter of the main letter, or what might not edify. In these accessory letters, anyone may quickly write what an overflowing heart will tell, in orderly fashion or without order. But in the main letter this may not be: it must be written with special and edifying care, so that it can be shown and edify. (BU, 83)

The difference between the main letter and the accessory letter was so important to the first Jesuits that a nickname was found for the latter. The accessory letter acquired the name "hijuela," "little daughter" among the confreres — perhaps because such a little daughter could be somewhat more relaxed and behave herself somewhat more spontaneously, more naturally, more directly, and more in a spirit of friendship than the main letter, the one intended for a larger public. So much for an unspectacular explanation of the formulation "the Jesuits' little daughters."

Ignatius regarded the distinction between the two kinds of letters as anything but casual or amusing. It cost him much effort and nervous energy. He once wrote: "You need write only to one, and I must write to everybody. I can truthfully say that, last evening, we determined that the number of the letters that we send everywhere was up to 250. And even though all in the Society are kept busy, I am convinced that, even if I am not that busy, I am no less so than anyone, and that with less physical health" (BU, 84) — a passage that expresses his personal burden, an urgent request, a bit of irony, and his suffering from the often critical state of his health.

Ignatius had waged his most strenuous battle over the culture of letter-writing with one of his first companions, Nicholas Bobadilla. In a mixture of earnestness and irony he offers him the office of general if he thinks persons in the General Curia in Rome have more time to write letters than he has in his assignment in Vienna, or if he believes that a different style ought to be cultivated there (see BU, no. 97).

The battle over correspondence constituted one of Ignatius's most difficult educational measures. But on this point he did not yield. When he recognized something as really necessary, he could not be dissuaded from it. And he seems to have known that without communication there was no organization, and without communication and organization there was no community.

Chapter 8

Helps for the Learning Process of Communication

Ignatius would not be Ignatius had he known only a theory of the practice of communication and no helps for its practice. A series of such fields of exercise and aids for dealing with them — most of them from Ignatius himself, some only in his spirit — must be given at least a minimal presentation. It is clear, meanwhile, that the actual help consists not in the presentation of the exercise, but in the exercise itself.

Playing Language Games: "One Word Leads to the Next"

A Swabian, who was awkward verbally and otherwise, had suddenly fallen head over heels in love. So he decided to take counsel of his family as to how he could have a conversation with his beloved, who up until this time knew nothing of her good fortune. The family felt that things wouldn't be nearly as difficult as he thought; and finally his father encouraged him: "One word leads to the next!" This meant, of course, that the one newly in love should go to the girl, simply begin to speak, and then the play of conversation would be under way. So he went off, and returned. To judge by his report, the conversation must not have gone well. The reason why came to light: the would-be lover recounted that he had gone and said to the young woman, over and over again, the recommended formula: "One word leads to the next, one word leads to the next, . . . " but that the girl, despite

126

many repetitions, had not taken the bait, and no conversation had taken place.

Apart from the fact that Swabians are of course not as simple as this story would have it, and apart from the fact that this is a paradigm of a classic misunderstanding, it becomes clear to the open-minded reader that speech is a tool for dealing with one another, and a person can handle this tool skillfully or unskillfully. Our speech, our idiomatic expressions, our tone, often enough determine the happy or unhappy course or outcome of a conversation.

The positive side of this fact is that our work with and on speech can yield much in the way of a successful communication. Ignatius knew this quite precisely. A person who, like him, in the years of his formation, wished to live and move in the diplomatic, courtly world without committing too many faux pas, had to become acquainted with courtly speech and courtly etiquette. There are some delightful episodes that show how he used the tool of speech. We have one of them from Father da Câmara's *Memoriale*. Da Câmara describes how Ignatius dealt with persons in different ways, on different levels, and how in doing so he altered his use of words.

> And so, when our Father first deals with someone, he tells him everything at once, and speaks with him in a manner such that, even if he were very imperfect, he could take no offense. Later, when he has gradually come to know him better, and as he himself acquires influence, he gradually begins to take liberties with him, so that, without having a sense of any violence being done to him, he changes, he changes the whole game. For example: A doctor of theology comes to the Society, let us say, a Father Olave, and our Father first calls him "Reverend Doctor" and "Your Grace." Then he drops one of these. Then he leaves it at "Doctor." Then he just uses his name. And so he says, "Reverend Doctor Olave, would Your Grace...." Then "Doctor Olave, would you...." Then "Olave...." (MEVI, no. 107)

A story like this can be read simply as an amusing anecdote, but it serves just as well to put a question to myself: How sensitive am I to the language to be used in the interplay of encounter? How consciously do I handle the tool of language? Do I use the opportunities that lie in a conscious conversation format?

Perhaps an aging married couple could supply us with an example of the effort on the part of two persons more than eighty years old to work on language and improve their communication. Again and again the two had suffered misunderstandings. "But I said that!" "No, you didn't!" "I did too!" "No, you said exactly the opposite!" After this interplay of language had come to the same dead end time after time, the two finally decided, for the future, to end the useless back-and-forth with this sentence: "One of us is mistaken." And so even the truth of the fact that someone is mistaken can become a ground of mutual understanding. One should not believe that one is "too soon too old" for such learning.

Turns of Phrase as Turn of Conversation

I once had a key experience that made me appreciate the liberating power of turns of phrase and that has been a help to me to this day. I was with a group of college students, where it constantly happened that one or the other, with his sharp tongue, would mow down what the others wished to say as if with a scythe. I often felt my own words stick in my throat. But then I observed with astonishment how one of the participants in the conversation remained calm, looked around the group in friendly fashion, and, as if it had been completely obvious, explained, "Oh, I see that completely differently!" This turn of phrase usually made it possible for the conversation to go on. I have adopted this sentence, with slight variations, in my vocabulary. "I have had a different experience there." "Something else occurs to me instead"; "I see this somewhat differently than you." And astonishingly, this usually helps me not to feel a tightening in my stomach, and I can join the conversation once again.

In recent decades, a series of phrases or speech rules have had a certain vogue and have entered the speaking habits of not a few persons. Perhaps the best-known speech rule is the one regarding "I": "Say 'I,' not 'one' when you are speaking of yourself." "I feel this in such and such a way. . . . " "I don't know how to make any headway. . . . " "I should like this or that." What philosopher Martin Heidegger has said in his celebrated critical statements on the anonymous "one" as characteristic of our time has been adopted, as it were, in the simple rule of "saying I." This can help to dismantle anonymity, namelessness, facelessness.

Another popular linguistic image in the German-speaking world is the expression, "I'm not going to put this shoe on." This addresses the experience that "one" is occasionally (directly or indirectly) accused of things, and that one occasionally accepts them without realizing it, and takes them to be correct. In this way, one does oneself an injustice, instead of coming right out and saying: "That's not right! I experience and do and interpret this differently! I'm not going to put this shoe on!"

The experience that cultivating language makes life easier for oneself and others might raise the question in one's mind: "Why did we learn language only as children and young persons? Why don't we handle the instrument of language more carefully as adults? When one studies a foreign language, one has to learn not just individual words, but whole phrases, typical turns of expression, in order to be at home in the foreign language. Would it not be worthwhile to enrich our vocabulary by more consciously picking up the idioms of loving encounter and really practice using them? Should we as adults forbid ourselves to learn something new and leave that to children?

"We Are Worlds Apart": Simplicity in Speech

Place and time: the end of an exhausting oral examination in a Jesuit university, Department of Philosophy. At the end of the difficult examination, one student, in taking leave of the examiner, made the concluding observation: "Professor, we are worlds apart."

Presumably this story found such an echo among students, because it focused in on many a student's feelings. Besides, it voices a general experience of many persons, namely, that we live in different worlds, with different languages and thoughts: the world of the professions, the world of the politicians, the world of the teachers, the world of the laborers, the world of believers, the world of "children of this world," the world of the poor and the world of the rich, the world of scientists and the world of the laity. Persons who, on a tourist beach or at a folk festival, meet "persons from another world," or who happen upon a periodical for academicians, or a magazine for children, notice how very different are our languages — so different, that it sometimes seems as if understanding is nearly impossible.

Ignatius knew of these different worlds from his own experience. He came from the world of the nobility, the world of the court, and throughout his life came in contact with kings, ambassadors, bishops, diplomats, scholars. But he had just as many encounters with soldiers, simple women, prisoners, the homeless, and prostitutes. He knew and believed that this, too, was the "society of Jesus": Jesus of Nazareth moved among tax collectors and carpenters, wealthy women and poor widows, Pharisees and "the people that understand nothing of the law." Jesus — described in the Gospel of John as the "word made flesh" — wished to speak to everyone. This is why we hear him ask, again and again, "To what shall I liken the Reign of God?" And we hear that he spoke largely "in parables" to people. This was a language understood by all, the simple and the learned.

This intelligibility in communication is a great concern of Ignatius too, as expressed in a particular vow taken by Jesuits. In general, people know only that the Jesuits, alongside the "usual" vows of poverty, chastity, and obedience, also make a special vow of obedience to the pope. This vow is cloaked in some mystery by the fact that it is made in the sacristy after the public celebration. The point, however, is not some shadowy, secret agreement, but, together with the declaration of readiness for missionary assignments by the pope, it is a vow to "be there" for the so-called *rudes*, simple persons, those with little education, for young persons, for "the average person," for the "people." Jesuits were not only the sometimes notorious court confessors of kings, but just as much, or even more, the "priests of the people." The only ones who can "get to" and be with the "people" are those who, in Martin Luther's words, look "the people in the mouth" and look into their heart. Ignatius reminds his followers of this concern in many ways: He calls attention to the fact that, in this respect, one can learn much "from the more recent ones" — that is, from the Protestant preachers. He repeatedly sends the men in training to catechize children. He himself stood with his confreres in the marketplace in northern Italian cities and waved the people together with his cap, to speak to them in simple Italian. He steadfastly insisted that letters to the confreres be written clearly and understandably and himself wrote many letters several times over.

As disciples of Ignatius, the Jesuits had children learn the truths of faith in easy, catchy songs, and Peter Canisius wrote a simple catechism that for centuries served as the foundation for religion lessons in grammar schools. In Jesuit churches, the paintings and statues served as a Bible for the poor, who could not read or write. Theatrical presentations, as well, with hundreds of players, sometimes continuing for days, served the purpose of "popularizing" the message of faith.

In our highly complicated world of today, the concern for intelligibility and simplicity has gained a new meaning. How is democracy — participation of the many in decision-making — to be lived, when the speech of politicians, of the socially committed, is unintelligible? Surely there is no escaping the fact, above all in our "highly developed civilization," that there is and should be technical language, jargon. But without constant concern for intelligibility, complex events and decisions become ever more opaque and bring the danger of manipulation by those who enjoy a monopoly on technical language. Talk shows have their importance. To be sure, "journalism" must continually be criticized for oversimplifying and sensationalizing events. Yet, it has its task. How can a politics "for the people" be practiced if no one pays attention to the language of the people?

And doesn't the same thing hold true, in an altogether special way, for theology and the church's preaching? If certain popular religious books see so many printings, that's not primarily because their authors seek to spread welcome heresies everywhere, but because these books address theological and at the same time human questions and desires in a more understandable language than that of most theologians. The renewal of proclamation means first of all a renewal of language. A renewal of preaching seeks connection with reality, connection with persons, simplicity. Connection with persons means speaking to persons out of the encounter with persons. "And the Word became flesh and lived among us," says the Gospel of John (1:14). Wherever a simple word of proclamation takes up residence in a human house, and persons who hear receive it, they will say: "We cannot keep from speaking about what we have seen and heard" (Acts 4:20).

"We Should Praise...": The Power of Positive Speech

I recall how an elderly sister once said to me, "Father, you have no idea how they celebrated my fortieth anniversary in the order, what they all said by way of praise and honor, hard to believe! If they had only spread it out over the last forty years, instead of saving it up for now!" This deep sigh, from the depths of the heart, says a great deal. It especially says how important recognition and praise are for a person. To put it another way, we may well say: Praise is to human development and maturation what the sun is to the growth of plants. The plant does not live on dew and water alone. It needs them. But it also needs light and sun and warmth. Human beings blossom when recognition and praise are bestowed on them. Persons discover strengths, talents, possibilities in themselves that they never dared to dream of.

The reverse test confirms this experience. How much courage for life, joy in life, and vitality can be lost, when what we do and how we present ourselves is criticized and sniggered at all around us! Many persons give up. True, there are children and young people who drive themselves to the highest achievements, although their elders show their dissatisfaction with good, even near-perfect, achievements in school. Not enough! Not for *their* daughters and sons, who, "it goes without saying," should do *perfectly* well. The maximum with such parents, teachers, and supervisors counts as the minimum. But don't even ask what psychological tension people suffer from when they constantly have to live and work in this kind of atmosphere. For healthy growth, the soul of the human being needs praise and recognition. Granted, these must be honest. When only a "pedagogical," strategic praise is bestowed, it usually means little. Can't you honestly say, "You've done a great job!" when someone raises a poor grade to a somewhat better one? This can be a considerably greater achievement, objectively, than when an A is raised to an A-plus. Praise belongs primarily where subjective progress has been made, not just where some objective norm of achievement has been met.

Words of praise are important not only for individual persons, but also for a whole community, for the atmosphere in a society, for the life of the church. This becomes very clear in Ignatius's rules for "thinking with the church." Here we find the formula "We should praise..." repeated ten times. To be sure, many things are listed as praiseworthy — papal calls to crusades, for example — that give today's Christians questions, if not qualms. But one thing remains perfectly clear: a community can live only on the basis of thankful approval. Granted, dissatisfaction and "constructive criticism" can be important factors for growth. But when everyone does nothing but criticize, then nothing, and no one, can stand up under it. When dissatisfaction "with each and every" person, thing, and factor has the upper hand over a long period of time, then any community — from the golf club to the political party, from the church to the state — collapses.

To be sure, it is not enough simply not to criticize someone constantly. It is too little to agree to "say something when something doesn't suit you." There is need for the repeated expression of thanks and praise in order to stimulate and improve vitality. One can easily and quickly notice in a factory, in a community, how creativity, or creativity *and* productivity, increase when a healthy "working climate" prevails. Surely this depends in good part on whether persons and their activity get noticed by way of respect, gratitude, and praise. As the anecdote at the beginning of this section shows, it need not always be a matter of a congressional motion. The everyday "Thanks!" or "Great!" or "Excellent!" or a friendly glance may suffice. Generous praise is the oil in the gears of everyday living.

And — it is important to see this — praise is not important only as a help to "maximization of income." It would be too little always to "endorse" one another only for the sake of a better attainment of goals set. For Ignatius, for the believing religious person, gratitude, praise, and appreciation belong to the essence of the human being, and not only to an interpersonal conversational strategy. "The human being is created to praise..." writes Ignatius in the "First Principle and Foundation" of the Exercises — made to "praise God," but surely other human beings as well, the creature of the God who has "made all things good." A reflection of this "making" resides in every human being. And how can human beings really praise God when they constantly criticize God's creatures, God's sons and daughters? ("You're okay, but your kids!...")

The Hats of the Jesuits: Forthright Criticism

In a score of places in his *Memoriale*, Father da Câmara talks about a hat. What he has in mind is not the old, three-cornered biretta, but the hats that Ignatius personally dealt his confreres. What is meant are sharp admonitions, which, with all his loving qualities, he uttered on many an occasion. He could certainly give a person a "tongue-lashing."

One of the best "hat stories" bears on a way of speaking that particularly rubbed Ignatius the wrong way. Da Câmara reports:

> One thing, one way of speaking, he could not abide, not only on the part of those of the house, but even on that of externs. It was when they spoke as if they were uttering a decree, as if, for example, we were to say: "This or that must necessarily be done," "There's no way to correct that but...." "The truth is this," and other similar ways of talking. And those who applied them, our Father called "decretalists," and, as I say, reproached them. And it seemed to him so undesirable to speak in this way that he even reprimanded a very important envoy, who was a friend of the Society and very well disposed to us in Rome. He would come to our house and speak in this way. The pope had to do this or that; and it was necessary that this cardinal do something else; one thing is obviously missing; or, someone must have this done; and so on. And on this basis our Father would answer him in the same manner, in that he counseled him concerning matters of his office, or recalled them to him. And he told us afterward, "Since he himself is a decretalist, he will have to listen to a few decrees from others." (MEVI, no. 204)

"Ignatius to the core!" would perhaps be too "decretalist" to say, but we can certainly see that this story sheds a lot of light on the man, his manner, his view of communication, and his dealings with persons. If all decretalists had to wear a hat, most hat-racks would doubtless be too small for many conversations.

"I'm Just Along for the Ride": Spiritual Counseling

Ignatius repeatedly referred to himself as a "pilgrim," that is, as someone on a journey. Often enough he was "alone and on foot," as he writes. But just as frequently he traveled with companions and found them a help or was a help to them. Often enough his traveling companions were chance acquaintances of a few hours, although they were also, on occasion, comrades of long years. The experience of companionship later broadened, in manifold ways and in the most varied connections. On his pilgrim's journey, Ignatius found spiritual company and, far more often, afforded it to others. In his quest for a spiritual counseling, he leaves us, in his *Pilgrim's Report,* a highly revealing narrative.

> Still in Barcelona, before he set sail, he sought out, according to his custom, all persons with experience in the spiritual life, in order to speak to them, even if they lived far out from the city in some village. But neither in Barcelona nor in Manresa could he, in all of the time that he spent there, find anyone who could have helped him as he himself would wish. At most, that woman from Manresa, spoken of above, the one who told him that she prayed to God that Jesus Christ would appear to him, only that woman, then, in his opinion, had penetrated the spiritual life somewhat more deeply. And so his anxious sense of urgency about a meeting with religiously interested persons had, after his departure from Barcelona, to be given up altogether. (BDP, no. 37)

Nearly every sentence of this account contains a message and shows:

- How important spiritual exchange was for Ignatius, so that, "according to his custom," he sought it everywhere, even "far out from the city."

- How, in such conversations, he was concerned not with theoretical discussion of things spiritual, but with "spiritual experience."

- How difficult it is to find someone with experience and sensitivity.

- How it had been a woman who obviously was able to tell him something.

- How he became independent, and how he got rid of his "anxious sense of urgency" that had characterized his quest: that is, he lost the anxious pressure "altogether," but not the joy of a good, helpful, spiritual conversation.

How Ignatius conceives of spiritual accompaniment is nowhere as evident as in the Exercises, when he describes the task of the one who gives the Exercises.

The basis for all the subtle ways of doing counseling is *simply being there* with the exercitant. A student once made this clear for me during my tenure as spiritual director in Rome by telling me a story. He told a story about little Karl who is sent off alone by his mother to buy groceries for the first time. Proud and fearful, he marches off, carrying a shopping bag, shopping list, and money purse. On the way, he meets his playmate Otto, who is a little older than Karl, and Karl asks him to come along, lest he himself have to "go it alone." Everything goes perfectly smoothly — the shopping bag is full, the purse safely stowed away, and Karl has even received a piece of candy. And the cashier leans across the counter and asks Otto: "Well, and you, what do you want?" Otto's brief answer is simply, "I don't want anything; I'm just along for the ride."

What this means for spiritual counseling is that the one who counsels does not determine the goal and the way, but with all his power and ingenuity he helps the one making the Exercises find the goal and the way. Merely being there is often the greatest help and says: You are not alone. Four eyes see better than two! I'll stay with you even when the going gets rough. I'll help you, if you wish, with my experience. It may be reaching very high, but is not entirely beside the point, to recall the "original name" of God: Yahweh means "I am the I-am-here." In the best case, accompaniment can reflect something of God's presence for human beings. This is of no little importance. Is it not almost everything?

Confession — Sacrament of Reconciliation — Discretion

One way of counseling that the Catholic Church offers a Christian on the way involves the "confessor," to whom one confesses one's personal guilt. The confessor is the witness of a yearning for forgiveness, reconciliation, and a new beginning. He provides a protected area, in which the darkest sides of life can be exposed. In particular, he brings Jesus' words to the present time: "Your sins are forgiven you." Much is expressed, and an important assurance given, with these words. They mean: "You are living again — so, live!" "Take up your pallet, on which you lie down there paralyzed in life, and go!" "You are again united to the community, accepted at the community table."

Granted, not every experience of confession reflects such situations of new beginning and reconciliation. Ignatius himself experienced this in his very depths. In one phase of his scrupulosity, which almost drove him to suicide, he ran from confessional to confessional until he was reduced to an inner zero. There he had an experience of redemption and abiding liberation. He had clearly and internally recognized that his spiritual perfectionism was destroying him and threatening to make him deviate from the discipleship of Jesus Christ and his path.

Throughout his life, Ignatius often called on the spiritual help of the Sacrament of Reconciliation. He was not always happy with his confessor. He even changed confessors once after his scruples had been overcome, although he was against frequent change. Father da Câmara characterizes the confessor whom he abandoned as being "of remarkable simplicity and inoffensive" (MEVI, no. 162). This was evident in that he "said certain things to the praise of our Father in such terms that it could have been an occasion of scandal."

This story makes clear, above and beyond Ignatius's understandable annoyance, that a relationship of trust lives on discretion. Without this "safe space," openness is impossible.

But Ignatius's experience with confession also shows how, despite this sacrament, which is in and of itself, a help to salvation, a person can become entangled in scrupulosity, or, at the opposite pole, smugness. The sacrament can be "for a fall." But it can also be the tale of that thankful consciousness of faith that came to expression one night in a deep sigh of Ignatius, which an eavesdropper overheard: "How infinitely good you are, O God, that you tolerate even a sinner like myself!"

"Ignatian": Syndicus, Admonitor, Collateral, Consultor, Supervisor

The words of our heading here could look "Spanish"; actually, however, they come from the Latin and the Greek, and are especially "Ignatian." Since specialized terms like "group dynamics" have become part of a normal educated vocabulary, an Ignatian slip into an all too technical "foreign language" is surely not so bad. Let's briefly mention the tasks involved in these "roles." They all show how seriously Ignatius took the helps to communication that were to be had through other people, through conversation and advising.

The Syndicus

The syndicus, the confidant, was supposed to pay attention to external matters, like the keeping of the rules of conduct, and then give his observations to the superior. This did not go extremely well, and so the institution was given up. Still, in many respects it was helpful while it lasted. A syndicus could be assigned to an individual, or someone could look for one himself, so that he might help him when he wished to improve himself with some manner of behavioral change. This counsel, one can safely, and often successfully, pass on: "If you want to improve in some matter important to you, then find yourself a person who has become your friend, and ask him whether you could not for some time every week, just briefly, recount how it is going with your proposed behavioral change." Five or ten minutes — a letter, a short telephone conversation, can suffice. "Listen: with my concern, my resolution, my project, it went thus and so this past week, and I should like to continue in this way or otherwise."

The helping person need by no means be very experienced in conversation, advising, or counseling. It's enough to listen, which in itself clears up many things for the speaker. And it is especially noteworthy that such conversations, held over a number of weeks or months, can be the best help for difficulties with continuity and consistency. Much in our plans, aims, and resolutions is fruitless because we only pursue them for a short time. The "check-up conversation in friendship" is about the best help for personal growth.

The Admonitor

The admonitor is the "warner," the "caller to attention." He is especially assigned to the superior general of the Jesuits, but is also responsible on the provincial level. In the "complementary norms" of the Thirty-Fourth General Congregation of the Jesuits, it is stated:

> He shall be a good member of the order, bound to God in prayer, of a reasonably advanced age, with good, mature judgment, practiced in our Institute and the affairs of the Society, with great zeal for our Institute, but at the same time with the gift of discernment, not naive and not overly reserved, such that one may expect that the superior general will gladly accept him; but the Admonitor is not to neglect, owing to any human respect, the duties of his office or the good of the Society. (SGJ, 433–34)

One may perhaps ask, after this description, whether it is even possible to find such a person. But in any case, it can make sense: It furthers the good of a community when there is someone who faces the superior as an authority figure himself, who advises him with benign criticism, and to whom one may apply at any time. I think of certain persons who had an ecclesial or societal responsibility and who came and recounted to me that they had most urgently asked a friend: "Please do me the service of letting me know if I slip up when I am no longer sufficiently on track, when I've lost touch with my grassroots. We can no longer see each other as often as before, but do me the service of friendship now, in this manner. If you hear criticisms from people, if you hear that I am high-handed and no longer open to suggestions, that I no longer listen and immunize myself from criticism — then at least please come to me and speak openly with me." It is a tragedy when, as sometimes happen, everyone knows "it" except the person involved. One must surely not be a major superior in the Society of Jesus in order to make mistakes and thus have need of persons who will point them out.

The Collateral

The collateral, that is, the one "at one's side," besides the task of critical instruction, also has that of collaboration. And so in the Constitutions we read that the collateral is to "take pains, insofar as possible, to bring the subordinates, together and with their immediate superior, to agreement, moving among them like an angel of peace" (SGJ, no. 661). Although this office existed only in the early Society, there is still need for an angel of peace, whether officially appointed or freely, without formal commission.

The Consultor

An important role is still played today by the panel of consultors. Their function is that of an advisory group. Former superior general Pedro Arrupe once recounted how differently he felt toward himself and his role, depending on whether he, as superior general, sat with his advisory organ, the panel of consultors, or he himself was called in by other communities in an advisory capacity. As adviser, he said, he could often express himself more freely, decisively, and creatively. For superiors, there are far more likely to be restraints to be considered in the form of supposed or actual realities, personal problems, financial questions, a need for discernment, and so on.

Supervisor, Practice Adviser, Practice Group

Today's customary form of supervision and practice-consultation was practiced by Ignatius himself. On occasion, he had his confrere da Câmara tell him every day how things were going with the counseling of an exercitant and gave him suggestions for how to carry it forward — surely one of the most effective aids to learning how to be a good adviser. Learning by practice counseling can be reinforced even more if a group regularly meets to exchange their experiences. Here discretion is one of the most important rules.

We may omit a treatment of how each of the various communication roles created by Ignatius was more or less effective for the interplay of communication among Jesuits. One thing is clear: Ignatius tried to promote the culture of decision and communication by many means. He seems to have been proved right in the event, and we could learn certain things today from not a few of the means he used.

Nothing More Open:
The Manifestation of Conscience

Must a woman being interviewed for a job tell the interviewer that she is pregnant? How much openness is obligatory? How much must be left up to the free and fair rhythm of conversation?

When Ignatius's Constitutions discuss the manifestation of conscience, the point is to have the greatest possible, freely chosen openness to one's superior. A readiness to speak of one's own weaknesses, strengths, preferences, ideas, crises, life situations, and so on finds its motivation in the effort to do one's best in the most effective service of the proclamation of the word. A text from the Thirty-Second General Congregation may clarify the meaning of this demanding "event":

> Both the superior who sends and the confrere who is sent have a greater certitude that a mission is really the will of God when a special conversation, or manifestation of conscience, has preceded the dispatch. For in the manifestation of conscience, the superior obtains an inner acquaintance with the subject, what this member of the order can do and what not, and what support he needs by way of advice or other helps in order to complete his task to the best of his ability. But the confrere learns the sense of the mission he has accepted and sees what he must do in order to do justice to his responsibility. The more complete and sincere a manifestation of conscience is, the more authentically we learn the will of God, and the more perfectly we come in spirit and in heart to that unity from which our apostolate draws its strength. If sincerity and a sense of community are wanting in mutual relations, then a community quickly petrifies either in purely formal structures, which no longer do justice to the demands of the time, or simply dissolves. (GK, 275–76)

The phenomenon, so demanding for all involved, of the manifestation of conscience can bear its fruit only if it occurs in the spirit of freedom, trust, discretion, and even love. When this manner of communication is in operation, a style of leadership can be lived that directs itself optimally to the individual and the common task.

Brotherly Reprimand:
Feedback and *Correctio Fraterna*

One need not have studied psychology or taken a course in group dynamics to have some understanding of what "feedback" means. To give someone feedback means to "report back" to him or her about how he or she as a person — in behavior, speech, and action — is affecting others as measured by their own feelings, perceptions, and judgments. When someone on the streetcar cries out, "Ow, you're stepping on my toes!" that person is in control of the basics of feedback, that is, he or she does not suppress the pain but "reports it back." Of course, this "person" could have reacted with, "Get off of my foot, you big clumsy jerk!" Then the probability of a little battle developing on the streetcar is greater than it would have been with the previous remark. And this again, ideally, could lead us to this insight: feedback involves not only the capacity to express one's sentiments, but also the necessity of cultivating one's own expressions in speech.

Augustine once expressed that "brotherly correction" — known in cloisters as *correctio fraterna* — is one of the greatest services a Christian love of neighbor can offer. Today, Augustine would certainly exchange this for a broader *correctio* — and no longer talk about merely a brotherly correction, if you please, but a "brotherly and sisterly correction." In many novitiates there used to be the so-called "Guardian Angel Service." In it two novices each called one another's attention to things each had noticed during the previous week. Sometimes this led to silliness and for the most part nothing except rather critical remarks, but no positive ones. Still, there was definitely helpful feedback as well. To put things positively: the question is whether we live in an echoless social space or in a space with good human acoustics.

In the key Ignatian text on communication, his letter to the three Jesuits who were traveling to the Council of Trent, the writer speaks expressly of a form of "social echo," feedback in community. The crucial statements stand under the head "In Order to Help One Another More":

> Some evening, let one ask all the others to correct in him what they think they should; and the one corrected is not to contradict, but neither is he to be required to give an account of the matter in which he has been corrected. A second is to do the same thing on another evening; and

so on, that all may help one another to greater love and greater fragrance for all sides. (BU, 115)

Surely one could translate "fragrance" in this text as "good atmosphere" or "good repute." Surely one could read the word "correct" as denoting something all too "schoolmasterly." But those who approach the text with a modicum of good will are sure to see at once that "brotherly correction" is here presented in a good sense and is regarded as helpful for growth in the capacity for communication.

There is the temptation to write, here again, in an exclamatory style. What importance communication and its cultivation have here! How very much is this seen as a process that needs careful perception and practice! How clearly we are shown here that, from beginning to end, the point is not smooth functioning, but the cultivation of a good atmosphere and the growth of loving encounter! And finally, what experiential knowledge is expressed in this rule, which asks for feedback and asks the subject not to comment on it at once with objections and excuses, but first and foremost to perceive it attentively.

Surely we may permit ourselves to fantasize a bit and ask: What would become of councils, synods, provincial congregations, parish council meetings, bishops conferences, caucuses, etc. if it was part of their style that the participants should try to cultivate their interaction in this way!

True, such a procedure demands inner prerequisites. No basic mistrust may prevail among the participants, and they must be ready to agree on certain constructive "rules" for feedback. Among these tried and true rules are:

- The feedback has to be wanted by both sides.

- The feedback should be phrased concretely. That is, it must relate to exactly describable situations: "That time, yesterday, when you slammed the door.... When you said to me, 'Damn you!'... When I ask you a question and you just don't answer,..." and so on.

- The feedback must relate to a time period of the recent past, memories of which will still be green.

- The feedback must be given from one's own personal experience, and this without interpretations, explanations, and evaluations. Expressions like, "That triggers in me,... That reminds me of,... Here are my feelings on that,... The feeling, the question, the impression comes to me... " can be helpful.

- For receiving feedback, it is important just to listen attentively, or at most ask for a clarification when something has not been exactly understood. Such a question must be a matter not of justification, but only of perceiving the feelings of the other and the effect of one's own behavior on the other.

- Feedback requires sufficient time and leisure, with a break afterward so that it can be digested.

- Afterward, there can be feedback on the feedback — a "reporting back" on what the original feedback has meant to someone.

The individual rules — whether to be applied in a one-on-one situation or in a group or board meeting and so on — should be looked for and agreed upon together, after it is clear to all concerned what creative feedback is all about and what it is definitely not at all about (simply to afford a means of ventilating pent-up vexation, even though such conversations can be helpful for this as well). Nor is it about wanting to remodel a person according to our own "image and likeness." Instead it's a matter of the listener's experiencing how his or her own behavior affects others, and the feedback-provider's doing the other a service with a view to the personal growth of both.

At this point, it will be worthwhile to take certain further points into account.

- Feedback conversations need not always be officially arranged. What is important is that the daily intercourse of the participants naturally ought to occasion feedback as to what is pleasing, what occasions difficulties, what is helpful, and so on.

- At the same time, it can be helpful to build the habit of an occasional look back at how persons affect one another and to speak not only of work, but also of how the persons in the conversation get along. With such regular conversations the level of inhibition is continuously lowered, and one doesn't always have to begin by jumping over a hurdle, as often happens when one arranges an extra feedback session, because otherwise the "basin will overflow." Then one has a feeling of impending doom, and fear reduces the capacity to listen openly.

- What we usually overlook — nor is this to be found even in Ignatius's instructions — is that we may and should report the positive impressions and feelings that we have. After all, we do not always fail to get along with our fellow human beings. Often enough, they also give occasion for gratitude and approval! What Ignatius not infrequently did, and what was surely effective, was to say to one of two persons whom he knew or had befriended something good about the other, knowing that it would surely get back to the latter. An effective form of this indirect positive feedback: "Ignatius told me yesterday that your sermon struck him as excellent, and that the Spanish envoy had reported to him the same thing." Indirect feedback like that is like "ointment for the head."

Part of the reason for the frequent reserve manifested with regard to feedback may be that often the only institutional form of feedback in religious orders was negative: the "chapter of faults," in which members of the community confessed their faults before the others. I still remember what we called the *lapi-*

datio, or "stoning," as it was practiced in the novitiate. Here the kneeling novice, surrounded by twenty of his confreres, heard from the latter only negative things that they had observed about him, for half an hour. Surely this could be ranged in the category of hard training, but it was only half of the truth about a person. Human beings live not from their faults or consciousness of their faults, but from the entire truth of their lives and their persons.

In the most recent edition of *Praktisches Lexicon der Spiritualität* ("Practical lexicon of spirituality"), brotherly and sisterly correction is handled under "Criticism, Constructive." Feedback should be exclusively constructive, positive, and life-building! This imperative is right in the etymology of the word, since "feedback" literally means "nourish back," and therefore to receive and return nourishment. Surely feedback does not mean just speaking with a honeyed tongue, but neither, most emphatically, does it mean that "everybody gets their come-uppance." In biblical terms, feedback does not mean seeing the mote in the eye of the other and not the plank in one's own (see Matt. 7:1–3): rather it means bestowing on one another the gift of reciprocal recognition.

Taming the Tongue: Complaining in Writing

In a very graphic passage, the Apostle James speaks in his letter of the difficulty and necessity of taming, restraining, the tongue.

> If we put bits into the mouths of horses to make them obey us, we guide their whole bodies. Or look at ships: though they are so large that it takes strong winds to drive them, yet they are guided by a very small rudder wherever the will of the pilot directs. So also the tongue is a small member, yet it boasts of great exploits.
>
> How great a forest is set ablaze by a small fire! And the tongue is a fire. The tongue is placed among our members in a world of iniquity; it stains the whole body, sets on fire the cycle of nature, and is itself set on fire by hell. For every

species of beast and bird, of reptile and sea creature, can be tamed and has been tamed by the human species, but no one can tame the tongue — a restless evil, full of deadly poison. With it we bless the Lord and Father, and with it we curse those who are made in the likeness of God. From the same mouth come blessing and cursing. My brothers and sisters, this ought not to be so. (James 3:3–10)

The reality addressed here so powerfully and graphically by James is painful. How many persons in national, regional, and local politics are destroyed by rumor! How many suffer from false rumors, uncontrollably repeated and exaggerated with relish! "Have you heard? So and so has done or said such and such?" How many judicial proceedings there are, and how many official denials are made, in order to set right the facts of a case, statements, and so forth! How difficult it is to free oneself from a particular reputation. "If you throw enough mud," we say, "some of it will stick."

Ignatius was obviously aware of this and was so much against the repetition of negative stories about persons that it was said of him: "The Father never believes any of the ill spoken of anyone, not even by Polanco" (MEVI, no. 358), meaning that he would not "buy" sight unseen any negative statements about people even from his secretary, his right-hand man, who drafted most of his letters. And as with many other things, Ignatius committed such material to writing, "so that one might tell, more calmly and without passion, what he knows or has heard" (ibid.).

How the atmosphere of a community would change, if it were made a rule that when I pass on something negative about someone, then I must have good and demonstrable grounds for doing so. Would this not be a fruitful "checkpoint question": Why do I now — and perhaps often — speak to others about a person, and not first — if at all — to the person and with him?

The restraining, the taming of the tongue — this would be an ideal case for the "special examination of conscience," that is, for a personal behavior therapy, where one is one's own therapist. Surely Ignatius would counsel someone who notices that his tongue is sometimes like a "poisoned arrow" to live with it for weeks and months, every day, and give himself a written account of his progress. The necessary motivation could be the wish for better communication, a less polluted atmosphere, a more pleasant work climate. For James, it was ultimately a spiritual reason that supplied the deciding stroke: it is a contradiction to praise God with the same tongue with which one curses one's fellow human being, God's creature. This is a a frequent accusation made against many especially pious churchgoers. (Is it always justified? One ought to have it in writing, and even then it may not always be correct!)

Three-Party Conversation

You are in a most unpleasant situation when you have the vague feeling that someone is talking about you behind your back. For Ignatius this was really a thorn in his side. This is why he made confreres confront one another when an oral or written report of such a negative situation had been reported to him. He saw this as the duty of a physician, as it were, for the state of the community health; "He takes care that they confront one another, and never leaves a sore festering, without bringing it to light, except *ad tempus* (temporarily) with certain almost incurable cases" (MEVI, no. 359).

There are certainly situations in which one must continue to wait, because the "suppuration" is not yet "ripe" enough, or because it calls for a delicate preparation. But the normal case should be that one speak about difficulties directly and with one another. The contrary, the refusal of direct communication, bears the burden of proof that this is the way to proceed.

Direct confrontation is very much a concern in biblical spirituality. In the Latin derivation of the word "confrontation," we see the meaning that two persons show each other their "foreheads" (Latin, *front-*), their faces. After the Fall, God asks Adam, "Where are you?" Before Cain's murder of his sibling, after having rejected Cain's offerings, Yahweh asks him, "Why are you angry, and why has your countenance fallen? If you do well, will you not be accepted?" (Gen. 4:6–7). And a concrete turn of phrase for the endangered relationship between Yahweh and his people Israel is found in the words: "They have turned their backs to me, and not their faces" (Jer. 2:27). The way to redemption is the way of open encounter. Paul describes the ultimate fulfillment with words to the effect that "then" we shall see not only in enigmatic sketches, and as if in a mirror with an untrue surface, but "face to face" (1 Cor. 13:12).

There is one confrontational conversation that Jesus positively provoked among his disciples. He asks the returning disciples what they have been disputing as they walked along their way (see Mark 9:33–37). "They were silent, for on the way they had argued with one another who was the greatest" (Mark 9:34). Jesus' question must have been painful for the disciples. Perhaps it seemed to them, as it were, hypocritical of Jesus to have asked the question. Why was he asking precisely today, and not yesterday, when they might possibly have been speaking of how they would unreservedly give their lives for their Lord? However any of this may be, one thing is obvious: Jesus has openly addressed the question of the allotment of power and he also supplied a clear direction in which to pursue it: You are not to be like the lords of the world in their concern for positions of power, from which, once they are established, they subjugate others. The point is to engage all of your power and might in encountering one another humanely, constructively, helpfully, in the spirit of service, in the spirit of enhancement of life.

A three-way confrontational conversation can be a good help to the "enhancement of life." I recall a good conversation, many years ago, when three persons, including myself, were on a trip that lasted several hours. Interiorly, and exteriorly as well, I was in the middle and had nothing to do except see that each of the two might be able to speak his peace in calm, that questions addressed not be prematurely sidetracked, that "everything" get discussed. Surely not all problems between the two were resolved, but at least some good help for mutual understanding was provided. It is beautiful when you can at least catch a glimpse of yourself out of the corner of your eye. The three-party conversation can be a help in doing so.

On the Road to Emmaus

Before holding a three-party conversation, a tête-à-tête is normally in order. Here — especially in muddled situations — it can be useful to observe some rules.

1. The first and most important rule is that one of the partners only listens. Half an hour, an hour, two hours. At most, the "silent partner" may ask for a clarification of meaning. This is important. Otherwise conflictive conversations often enough produce only an escalation of self-justification, as each partner strives to shift all of the blame on the other, and everything becomes worse than before.

2. The one who speaks must recount only how he or she experiences the situation, the relationship. It is a matter, then, not of assigning blame, of judging, but of the subjective experience: "When you say such and so or do such and such, I get a stomach ache for the next three hours, . . . I lose sleep over it, . . . it occurs to me, . . . I wonder. . . . "

3. After each report of this kind, a few minutes' silence may ensue. It may be that something else may come to mind in the interval.

4. After a few days, the participants may exchange roles. The auditor of the previous day now shares his or her experience, while the other listens.

5. If the participants have a great deal of time, or when they are not having a very intensive, or perhaps their first, discussion of a problem, the role-exchange may take place on the same day, following the first part of the conversation — to be sure, only after a certain "digestive pause."

6. It is often helpful if the partners in this kind of one-on-one have their "conversation" while taking a walk. Many things are more easily solved in this way. It seems exaggerated when Blaise Pascal says that any problem can be solved by walking; but there is some truth in his declaration. For example, for the secret talks between Palestinians and Israelis, in Norway, at the resumption of the peace process, a psychologically important factor was the fact that the participants shared repeated conversations while taking walks in a natural setting.

It was with such "walks" in mind that the heading of this section, "On the Road to Emmaus," was chosen. The reference is to the striking narrative of Luke 24:13–35, in which two of Jesus' disciples, in all but complete hopelessness after their Master's crucifixion, return to their home town, Emmaus. On the way, they encounter the risen Christ, who asks them the reason for their obvious sorrow. To the disciples' reaction — the question whether the stranger is the only person in all Jerusalem who does not know what has happened — he does not react in turn: "Stop! Back off! If anyone knows what's happened, it's me!"

No, he "plays dumb," and asks, "What, then? What, in your view, in your experience, has happened?" Now the disciples recount all their needs, all of their questions. This lays the groundwork for a wider view, and for them to be able to perceive, for an instant, the new presence of Jesus. For persons who believe, this happening on the way to Emmaus can stand in the background of a difficult conversation of their own, bearing on relationships. Here too it is sometimes a matter of the death and resurrection of a relationship, or at least its healing and health. In this sense, such a one-on-one can become a conversation of three, held in the presence of Christ, who is there in the Spirit.

When a direct conversation is not possible, it can often be a help to carry on such a conversation in one's fantasy, with an imaginary partner. Even when someone has died, and inner reconciliation is still in order, a trip to Emmaus can contribute. In particular, the first part of this journey will be possible, as we speak of our own inner experience, from the depths of our soul. Of course, it is to be recommended that a period of silence ensue while the partners listen to the invisible partner. It is sometimes possible to "hear" an answer out of the silence, out of invisibility. The experience of others, to which I can attest, may be encouraging: as on the road to Emmaus, persons can once again come into conversation with one another; persons for whom it had not been possible for years were able to enter into conversation with each other.

The Introductory Round

There are many ways of getting together in which an "introductory round" supplies a good basis for further conversation. All participants can take two, three, or five minutes to recount what's been important for them since the last meeting, or where they are "coming from" today, and what they would like to "let go of" in order to be "present" better. This can create a more personal atmosphere that will be helpful for continued conversation. Here it is important for the leader's role in the group that the time framework be precisely agreed upon and kept to, in function of the size of the circle and the time at the group's disposal. Otherwise this part of the conversation may get much too out of hand.

The Listening Circle

In not a few groups, in recent years, the "listening circle" has been in vogue. The aim here is, as Ignatius says, to "listen and learn." Although — or because — this style of communication is very simple, it can have very great, sometimes almost unbelievable, effects. It guarantees all the participants an opportunity to express themselves, in rotation, on a specified theme. Otherwise it can happen that persons of notorious verbosity and magniloquence will dominate the conversation, and important viewpoints will not be discussed, not everyone will be really involved, and the results produced will fall short of reasonable expectations. A community can have become so accustomed to taking part in such conversations of its spokespersons that the felt need of all to think of their own contribution is simply no longer there. Persons allow the discussion to play out before their eyes and ears as if in an arena — interested, bored, or even put off.

It may be encouraging to know that, merely by way of taking part in such "listening circles," conversations and decisions become possible that have not been possible for long years. The only task of the leaders is to see that everyone really has the floor in the course of the conversation. It is perfectly all right for there to be repetitions, and no one should believe that her or his own contribution is too unimportant to be worth expressing. To the joy of all young people from now to the end of the world, Benedict put in his rule that it is sometimes from the youngest and simplest that the most wide-ranging contributions can come.

It can often be meaningful to repeat a listening circle, for instance to hold a listening circle on a listening circle, with the question, "What have the things that I heard earlier, and have thought through in a digestive interlude, provoked in me by way of thoughts and reactions?" In this fashion, a great deal of life and experience can often be recalled that even the most intelligent and most experienced individual does not know. "Four eyes are better than two."

To be sure, such a procedure may be time-consuming when pressing decisions are on the agenda, but in the long run this kind of communications is "worth it" if it is engaged in the right place, at the right time, and in the right dosage.

The Culture of Decision-Making: Quest for Alternatives, Weighing the Pros and Cons, Balance of Feelings

Ignatius practiced the most varied models of decision-making: spiritual decision-making in community; decisions in a carefully selected group representing others; and more. A detailed presentation would require an ad hoc treatise on Ignatius's leadership and decision-making practice. As the latter is bound up extremely closely with the practice of communication, it may be in order, briefly at least, to name important elements of Ignatian decision-making. Even if only the few elements sketched immediately below are implemented, these can mean a quantum leap in a great deal of decision-making practice.

1. Normally, a problem is open to a number of different solutions. The first element in Ignatius's manner of decision-making, then, is to seek several alternatives. Then the space for thinking and acting is broader right from the outset.

2. The second step consisted in Ignatius's always having the participants talk out all possibilities, especially since he meant to investigate all arguments pro and con, for and against each of the alternatives proposed. Here it was clear, materially and psychologically, that it was not a matter of getting any one of the alternatives through — for instance, the subjectively preferable one. One thing alone was at stake: carefully to weigh everything and then to select the best possible behavioral alternative.

3. The third element — perhaps the one most neglected by "ordinary" decision-making bodies — consists of using prayer, conversation, and meditation to gain one's inner freedom from fears and preferences and fixed ideas. Trying to come to a decision without psychic elasticity on the part of the participants — Ignatius called it "indifference — without equanimity, without "committed composure" (Teilhard de Chardin), leads to a battle, to victory and defeat, not to free decisions and common achievement.

Hearing — Discerning — Responding

The simple, well-known steps, "see — judge — act," which received such broad currency at the hands of Cardinal Cardijn, founder of the Young Christian Workers, form an important basic schema in the quest for decision and fulfillment. Somewhat more akin to Ignatian parlance is the terminology of the "Community of Christian Life" in Germany: "hear, discern, respond." For Ignatius "discernment" is a basic process for arriving at an action-oriented decision.

For example, in a group in which a member would like to be helped by the others in making a decision, the following manners of procedure — sometimes called the common *révision de vie,* "review of one's life" — can be fruitful.

1. In the first step, seeing or hearing, the purpose is to approach reality. Here, questions like the following can be important:

   - What does a spontaneous description of the situation look like?

   - How did the question come up?

   - What persons (individuals, groups) are involved?

   - What reaction was occasioned in the person(s) involved?

   - What tendencies are recognizable?

   - What absolutely must be said in order to make the situation clear?

2. The step of discerning is taken next, in silence: one allows the information to have its effect and asks questions such as:

   - What especially strikes me?

   - Where do I still have questions?

   - What concrete facts and reasons have to be weighed in making the decision, and what weight do I assign them?

- Where do there appear to be tendencies more in the direction of freedom, communication, life, and love? And where do I see and feel tendencies that seem to lead more in the contrary direction of resignation, hypocrisy, truncation of reality, unfreedom, selfishness, and violence?

- Where are there signs of suffering, fear, hope?

- Which words, deeds, and questions of Jesus come to me spontaneously upon hearing what I do?

In a "listening circle," after a time of silent reflection, all participants convey what has occurred to them.

3. The third step is devoted to "response," to answering. Here too it is important first to perceive and to sort out in silence what has previously been said by the others in the listening circle. Here too a string of questions may come spontaneously to mind, with a clustering and goal-orienting effect:

- In what direction do I see one or more possibilities of response?

- At all events, what do I regard as important, regardless of what precise direction the concrete response turns into?

- What response seems to me more in keeping with the spirit of the Gospel, with Jesus' message?

- Where do I see consequences for those involved?

- What will be the effects on the environment, and what reactions are to be expected from it?

- What else should still be clarified?

- What could be helpful for the road ahead?

- Where do I still see difficulties?

- Who and what could help me along the way?

Again a listening-circle is set up, with opportunities for feedback that will help clarify things. The decision or the search for further clarification is the responsibility of the one who has brought up the question.

This model of a common cooperation in view of a decision may sound pretentious, but it has stood the test more than once. It is creatively practiced in groups that have already made a good deal of headway together. Experience has shown that this kind of "community quest" for a solution helps its members to experience the group's value even more.

Closely related to the steps of "hearing, discerning, responding" is a set of words that for some years now has been known in Jesuit educational institutions as the "Ignatian pedagogical paradigm": "experience — reflection — action." For this paradigm to be fully developed, five steps always have to be taken in pedagogical praxis: context, experience, reflection, action, evaluation. To put them as questions:

1. What are the surroundings, the situation, the inner events and presuppositions? In other words, what is the context of the pedagogical process?

2. How can people be helped to a holistic experience? Or how can such an experience be expressed?

3. How can handicaps and experiences be grasped, felt, and understood more profoundly?

4. How can newly acquired insight bear fruit in the determination to shape practically one's life, in commitment and service to people?

5. And how, finally, can one's own practice be reviewed, questioned anew, evaluated, and improved?

For various reasons the Jesuits were long considered among Europe's leading educators. One crucial factor here certainly was the sort of pedagogical dynamics expressed in these five steps.

Joint Evaluation

For Ignatius, one crucial help is the regular personal examination of conscience, the "prayer of loving attentiveness." In the case of longer conferences and decision times — but also, in many circumstances, in the everyday life of a community — the collective growth of a group will improve if it practices a joint evaluation of the day every day. In a religious context, the session begins with a short prayer, which looks on the day with the eyes of the Spirit of God, and thence toward the future, the way to come.

- The best beginning is a short period of silence as we allow the day and its particular events, encounters, conversations, and so on, to become present. What has occurred? How has it moved me? What have I set in motion or sought to set in motion? What do I have a good feeling about? Where do I feel blocked? Where do I have questions? What was an especially precious thing about the day to me?

- After a few minutes of silent reflection, each participant can share something of what he or she was struck by, going around the circle.

- After this, another silence is in order, in which the participants look at the day once more, but this time through the eyes of the others, and thus from a broadened viewpoint.

- Finally there can be a short prayer of petition and thanksgiving.

Whether the process unfolds in an explicitly religious context or in another, the intended result is the same: more clarity and more community, and thereby more common seeking and finding.

Exercises and Personal Evaluation of the Day

A reference to the Exercises as a help for growing in the capacity for relationship could of course have been made at the beginning. At the same time, the Exercises are not normally a help that stands at the beginning of a spiritual journey. The essentials concerning a connection between the Exercises and communication has already had its own chapter. Here we shall only make certain succinct observations.

But first let us refer to a testimonial from Ignatius himself on the importance and efficacy of the Exercises. In 1536 he wrote a letter to his former confessor in Paris and tried to motivate him to participate in the Exercises, "since it is by far the best, after all, that I can think, feel, and understand in this life, both so that the person can engage in self-help, and so that the person can be of use to himself and can bear fruit, and can help and be of use to many others" (GB, no. 655).

There are always persons who have the experience that the Exercises are among the best things in their lives. Often a fruit of the Exercises is that persons are helped both on their explicit way of faith and in their psychic growth, even though the maturation and healing of the mind was not the first and only goal of the Exercises.

When, for example, foundations of mistrust are dismantled, when human reconciliation occurs, bases for communication and encounter are then, so to speak, laid anew. And yet the Exercises are not a simple miraculous recipe, and normally it makes sense to try to profit first from weekends of meditation and Bible study, from abbreviated Exercises, from Exercises with community elements, from daily Exercises, and so on. Once we are on our way, we will feel when a next step is in order.

The quest for subsequent steps belongs, for Ignatius, to the ABCs of daily, wide-awake living: the examination of conscience, the evaluation of the day, and the "prayer of loving attentiveness" are a kind of "Exercises for daily life," the "Exercises in reduced format." Every day, the opportunity and obligation arise anew to "go to the world" more, to become more present, to be nourished by gratitude, to allow oneself to be reconciled and transformed, and to forge ahead in hope.

At the end of so many instructions and aids for the growth

of the capacity for communication, what else can be said than the ultra-Ignatian instruction: Do whatever suits you best and helps you most.

And perhaps it's fitting, after so much has been "brought to our attention," to quote the motto of Friedrich Bollnow: "The only road from knowing about to knowing how is — practice."

Chapter 9

Love Consists in Communication

The sentence that makes up our title is monumental and should be cited in its original Spanish: *El amor consiste en comunicación,* "Love consists in communication." And if we follow the sentence to the end, it reads: "Love consists in communication on both sides," *El amor consiste en comunicación de las dos partes.* This sentence could be celebrated with a High Mass and incense. To Ignatius, it is fundamental for the meaning of communication. Why? Because it stands at the final climax of the Exercises, in the "Contemplation for Obtaining Love," at the end of four weeks of Exercises. It summarizes what Ignatius is concerned about, first and last and above all, and this in all its details: love. And love consists in communication — *El amor consiste en comunicación!*

"More in Works Than in Words": Love in Action

Ignatius makes two preliminary remarks concerning his great and splendid "Contemplation for Obtaining Love." The first one says: "Love ought to manifest itself more by deeds than by words" (GU, no. 230), a typical saying for a collection of Ignatian aphorisms. Ignatius has less dexterity with words than with life. He knows how often words are only words, conversation only chatter, and promises empty promises. Therefore, in love what counts is action, living. This statement is easy to comprehend. True community means not that one constantly talks about community and relationship, but that one concretely lives community. Not uncommonly, talk of community is an expression of

163

the fact that a community is in crisis and that one is searching for a solution. Surely, talking about it periodically may be meaningful and necessary, but the decisive thing is what happens, what is lived, what is done.

Nonverbal communication, we might say, is the backing of verbal communication, as gold and goods are the backing of paper money. Jesus demonstrates this with an example, in one of his parables. He has us visualize a son who responds to the request of his father that he go and do something with "Yes, yes," but does not keep his promise. The second son at first says "No," and yet afterward does what is asked. Jesus' question about which son lives with his father in community is a rhetorical one, since the answer is clear, and the addressee responds: "The one who has done the father's will." Community happens when we are present to the other. Community happens where one gives another precious time, where someone responds to the desires and needs of another, where one shares one's life, pieces of one's life, with another.

Loving as Partnership

The formulation "where someone share's one's life with another" emphasizes Ignatius's second preliminary remark regarding the "love theme," which is:

> Love consists in a mutual communication between the two persons. That is, the one who loves gives and communicates to the beloved what he or she has, or a part of what one has or can have; and the beloved in return does the same to the lover. Thus, if the one has knowledge, one gives it to the other who does not; and similarly in regard to honors or riches. Each shares with the other. (GU, no. 231)

These words express the fact that the crucial point of love is communication and, within communication, the acts of sharing and imparting. Community lives out of the capacity to share. This becomes visible in a special way when one realizes that, underlying the word "partnership," is the Latin verb *partire,* to "divide," to "share." The word "partnership" has had a world-wide career over the last few decades. It has become one of the most important words in many languages for speaking of a relationship. The word's connotations normally are: a partner is one who is independent; partnership is shown when one person leaves the other free and takes him or her seriously. But people don't generally notice that the original sense of partnership is sharing. A partner is someone who can share. Whoever cannot or will not share is incapable of community.

In a marriage, a family, a relationship of partners, it is obvious that all have to be willing and able to share with one another: the room, the cake, the time, the conversation, the work. A humanitarian education will orient itself toward having all of its participants learn to share themselves, share with one another. Wherever there has been "separation from bed and board," you obviously have the termination of the community of sharing.

Not only in the family, but also in the larger society, sharing is a basic process. Involvement, participation, and concern are words fraught with political content. Shortly after the Wall dividing Germany fell and Germans started to come back together, with some difficulty, politico Lothar de Maizière uttered the memorable dictum: *Teilung wird nur durch Teilen überwunden,* "Division is overcome only by sharing." This is not only a clever formulation, deserving of a place on a calendar, but a profound life-truth, and one that applies to individual relationships as well as to groups and to states. Otherwise the growing tension between individualism and solidarity cannot be bridged or lived. Sharing is the lived solidarity and partnership of human beings. At a time when interpersonal relationships in families and throughout society are in danger, the capacity to share becomes a serious measure and test of community.

Love as Self-Communication

However appealing the formulation may be that love consists in sharing, an acutely sensitive person might nevertheless ask:

Does love really mean, at its core, only that one gives something, gives away something of oneself? Isn't that too little a concept? In the "Contemplation for Obtaining Love" it becomes abundantly clear that for Ignatius, this does not quite touch the core of love. He invites us to contemplate the blessings of God and of the divine creation:

> I will call back into my memory the gifts I have received —
> my creation, redemption, and other gifts particular to my-
> self. I will ponder with deep affection how much God our
> Lord has done for me, and how much he has given me
> of what he possesses, and consequently how he, the same
> Lord, desires to give me even his very self, in accordance
> with his divine design. (GU, no. 234)

Here it is stated with absolute clarity: all the gifts of love are "only" signs, as it were, of the fact that God wishes to make a total gift of himself, and does so. God's love is a total outpouring of the divine self into creation — "as much as he can."

This likewise makes it clear that the familiar devotional prayer — Ignatius's famous "Suscipe" — is not offering, but response. Only in view of God's incomprehensible self-giving does Ignatius make his offering:

> Take, Lord, and receive all my liberty, my memory, my
> understanding, and all my will — all that I have and pos-
> sess. You, Lord, have given all that to me. I now give it back
> to you, O Lord. All of it is yours. Dispose of it according
> to your will. Give me your love and your grace, for that is
> enough for me. (GU, no. 234)

If this prayer is a response to an antecedent self-giving on the part of God, then one could actually formulate a devotional prayer to be uttered by God, who "desires to give me even his very self":

> Receive, human being, my Yes to you in my embrace of
> your life. Receive, human being, my Logos, my Word of

Creation, in whom and for whom everything is created. Accept my loving desire for you. Take the gifts of creation, and create and work and invent with them. Receive, human being, my eternity: I wish to "make history" with you. Take, human being, my freedom in the captivity of Jesus. Accept my life, which leads to Jesus' death and resurrection. Give me, human being, only your love. That is enough for me!

At this point it will be appropriate to bring to mind one of the most important contributions of the great theologian Karl Rahner, who gave the theology of grace a new perspective. Rahner understands grace as God's "self-communication," thereby moving front and center the personal dimension of all grace-filled godly encounters. Grace is not a "grace-package," a "holy thing" which is given, but is, at its core, God's own self and self-communication. The Ignatian source of this view — which is not often recognized — is precisely the center of the "Contemplation for Obtaining Love," where "he, the same Lord, desires to give me even his very self, to the extent that he is able."

What is said here of the relationship between human beings and God holds true as well for encounters between human beings. Those who truly encounter others in a personal way wish to give not only "something" belonging to themselves, but themselves. Everything in a loving encounter becomes an expression of meeting "face to face" or "person to person."

Stages of Loving Self-Communication

Giving, and self-giving, in the communion of life knows various stages, colors, planes, dimensions — and roadblocks. The great philosopher of religion Romano Guardini, who was such an important personality for the liturgical movement as well as for an awakening sense of community in Germany's youth movement, once offered a retrospective description of his experience with the stages of community. In a first phase of enthusiasm, he and his new community had believed that community should mean sharing everything with one another. Later it became increasingly clear that such a community was too constrictive: community ought to mean understanding one another, even when they could not share everything with one another. And eventually a last stage opened out as the core of all community: respect for the life mystery of the other, the "you."

Depending on the starting point and the goal, there are different ways to name the stages of community. It is now fairly common, in discussing the developmental stages of a community, to use the distinctions of orientation phase, intimacy phase, struggle for power phase, and differentiation.

With Ignatius, important steps along the developmental path of community come to light, as far as the path of the Exercises is concerned, in the culminating "Contemplation for Obtaining Love." And what is valid for the path of an individual in the Exercises can be modified and, when transposed, can have meaning for a relationship of two persons or even a larger community.

"Longing Is the Beginning of Everything" (Nelly Sachs)

Without longing, without wanting, without desire, nothing is alive, and nothing comes into movement. Anyone not interested in anything, not open to others, not even sensible to the pressure of suffering in life, exists in a sort of twilight and isn't really alive. This sort of person is incapable of an encounter with reality, has not grasped the truth of the proposition, "All real life is encounter" (Martin Buber). For a lively connection, especially a friendship connection, to take place, an interested openness is necessary and must be awakened. Spanish philosopher José Ortega y Gasset once said, "Falling in love is a phenomenon of attention." Out of a group of people who are "all the same" to oneself, an individual emerges into the focus of attention of one's heart, becomes significant. Thus falling in love begins, an intensified connection. For things to go further, it is necessary to maintain attention and therefore to make time for each other.

In the prefatory remarks to the Exercises, this is thought of as gaining experience, preparing oneself, meditating, praying, a relishing of things from the inside, generosity, willingness to take risks, and time to take time. When such things are missing in a relationship, community cannot grow.

Love as the Meaning of Existence

Expressly or by implication, human beings are confronted time and again with the question of the meaning of their actions, their lives, and the meaning of all life. The answer in the Book of the Exercises sounds simple and grand at once: living by and out of God, toward God, and in God, and shaping one's own life freely in terms of this relationship.

There are three basic attitudes that show what gives meaning to life, encounter, and community: a life lived on the basis of praise, a life in awe, and a life of service (see GU, no. 23). This is said primarily about our relationship to God, but a glance at successful community validates the importance of these attitudes for intrahuman relationships as well. There is no community without indebtedness and gratitude, without recognition and praise. There is no community without awe of the mystery of life, or without respect for the dignity of the other. There is no community without "being-there-for-each-other," which means mutual service. Nothing shows the validity of these statements as much as the obverse: What destroys actual, true, successful community more than its not being experienced as a gift? What destroys relationships more than when others are not seen in their otherness, that is, are overlooked? Can a community come together, let alone grow, if everyone lives in an isolating self-centeredness rather than as part of a supportive "being-there-for-each-other"?

The statement of purpose in the Book of the Exercises (see GU, no. 23) emphasizes that if a life, if a relationship, a friendship means to grow, it is important to make sure that there is a common foundation, common values, common goals. Otherwise no common path can develop. Persons with different goals must walk different paths. More than a few relationships fail because they rest on a mere feeling of mutual attraction and not on an orientation toward a common goal of meaning.

Likewise, relationships often fail because, even though the partners dream together, fantasize together, they do not take steps toward a common realization of their dreams and fantasies. Ignatius stresses, when he states the goal of the Exercises, that the shaping, the "ordering" of life is a crucial matter (see GU, no. 21).

It is of special importance that the search for the realization of one's dreams take place with an inner freedom, "freedom of spirit," or "detachment."

When people consciously aspire to grow in their relationship, it will be a good thing for them to ask themselves every so often such questions as:

- What sort of meaning does our relationship actually aim to reach?

- Do we have common foundations and values?

- How do we experience the interplay of giving and receiving, of appreciating and being appreciated?

- Do we cultivate a respectful manner of encounter?

- Do we live the mutual "being-there-for-each-other"?

- How do we deal with freedom, and with fear, in our encounter?

- How do we live the tension between dream and reality in our encounter?

- Can we experience the otherness of the other in a positive way?

Life Means Reconciliation

Is there a human life or encounter in which one does not withhold from the other opportunities to grow? A life where one senses no insufficiency, no reciprocal guilt? There may be great differences between a crisis in a relationship and an open betrayal which aims at the destruction of the relationship. Jean-Paul Sartre's phrase, "Hell is other people," may be overused and may prompt the retort, "Heaven is other people." But it still contains a piece of truth and human life-experience.

The way of the Exercises — a path to the deepening of encounter — consciously leads into dark ravines, to the borders of one's own nature, the detours of one's own history, to the burdens of family history, to past trauma, to the depths of inferiority complexes and depression, into the "hell of egotism," into notions of meaninglessness and Godlessness, into terrible fears about oneself and strange fears about what each and every one of us desires most deeply: to love and to be loved.

Growth in community always has to deal with overcoming crises, with rejuvenation, healing, forgiveness, reconciliation. In the words of Marie Ebner-Eschenbach: "In the forgiving of the unforgivable the human being is closest to divine love."

"In Good Days and Bad"

Long before the divorce rate's "quantum leap," the Catholic wedding ritual contained a line in which the bridal pair promised to remain faithful to each other "in good days and bad." Here is almost a disturbingly dark patch of cloud in an otherwise rosy-hued wedding sky, but exactly for that reason a phrase that brings the reality of a relationship squarely into view. We humans, we Christians, know that a relationship can be exposed to heavy burdens. We see a unique possibility of growth in love when love tries, again and again, to master a crisis. By "love" we mean not only a fair-weather love, but one that tries to sail into a stormy wind as well. We come to know each other again and again as imposition, as challenge. We believe that our love becomes stronger on both sides when we walk our path together "in good days and bad." That — in spite of this — a shipwreck may occur in a human life does not detract from the meaning of the search for an "all-weather love."

In the Book of the Exercises, this is said of communion with Jesus Christ, but it holds likewise for any relationship. And it also holds for every relationship that falling in love is a "phenomenon of beginning," and that love is self-communication in a life community, a process of everyday living and practice.

"Love Is Strong as Death" (Song of Solomon 8:6)

A final intensification of love occurs in the face of death — when a dear person dies, when one's own life nears its end, when a love is challenged to love beyond the limit of understanding. The appropriate biblical verse says: "God so loved the world that he gave his only Son" (John 3:16). There could scarcely be a stronger expression of the bond of love than willingness to put one's life at risk or to give it up for another.

The text of an obituary notice seeks to describe the mystery of love and loving bondedness with these words:

> But soon we shall die, and all memory will then disappear from the earth, and we ourselves shall be loved for a little while and then forgotten. Yet that love will have been enough: all movements of love return to the One who has allowed them to come into being. Not even a remembrance is necessary in love. There is a land of the living and a land of the dead, and the bridge between them is love — the only thing that abides, the only meaning.

What is understood biblically and theologically as the mystery of faith, the mystery of dying and resurrection, is also the mystery of love that comes to completion in the end. Thus, the declaration that all true life is encounter may be reformulated: all true life, all true community, all true love is a dying and a resurrection, a letting-go and setting-free of life, in order to gain life. All of these words lie at the edge of unspeakable beauty and truth, and yet they can fade to become mere feast day talk, Sunday sermons, or calendar quotes.

The "Contemplation for Obtaining Love" visualizes love not only in its unfathomable depth, but also in its daily tangibility, with a God who is "love from on high," and yet who works and cares for us in the smallest detail and in every daily event:

> I will consider how God labors and toils for me in all the creatures on the face of the earth; that is, he acts in the manner of one who is laboring. For example, he is working in the heavens, elements, fruits, cattle, and all the rest — giving them their existence....
>
> ...I will consider how all good things and gifts descend from above; for example, my limited power from the Supreme and Infinite power above; and so justice, goodness, piety, mercy, and so forth — just as the rays come down from the sun, or the rains from their source. (GU, 236–37)

Words like these also illuminate what Marie Luise Kaschniz has said in her poem "Resurrection":

> Sometimes we rise up,
> rise up to the Resurrection
> in the midst of the day
> with our living hair
> with our breathing skin.
> Only the usual surrounds us
> No mirage with palm trees
> with grazing lions and gentle wolves.
> The alarm clocks don't stop ticking
> Their illuminated hands do not fade.
> And yet lightly
> and yet invulnerably
> ordered in a mysterious order
> anticipated in a house made of light.

Chapter 10

Communication with God

Prayer

Can we enter into a bonding with God? How does encounter with God happen? Is communication with God possible? What does communication with God look like? How do faith and life work together? These or similar questions are asked repeatedly by believing, searching, religious people.

Many ask the question about communication with God as a question about prayer: How can we pray? How should we pray? How does God answer our calling and questioning and praise?

Because prayer — to use Bishop Walter Kasper's expression — is regarded as a "faith emergency," the questions listed here about communication with God have a special significance. Ignatius's answers to these questions lead in many directions and carry a variety of messages.

"Allowing Oneself to Be Embraced": God in All

In the fifteenth preliminary remark of the Book of the Exercises, one finds what is possibly the most beautiful description of the goal of the Exercises. The counselor should leave the exercitant entirely free and not manipulate her on her way. By way of explanation, it would be "more appropriate and far better that the creator and Lord himself should communicate himself to the devout soul, embracing it with love, inciting it to praise of himself, and disposing it for the way which will most enable the soul to serve him in the future" (GU, no. 15).

174

This text has its charm and tenderness especially in the Spanish text. There, two phrases in particular make themselves heard. The Spanish indeed has ... *se communique* ... — our very theme and context. And second, with special tenderness: " ... embracing it with love. ... " In the divine embrace, human life is aroused. In the original image of connection, of embracing, *communio* takes place, community expresses itself. To speak here of a mere process of communication would be inadequate. Deep down, the Exercises are concerned with communication between God and human beings as an expression of loving community. And precisely that is Ignatius's concern in his entire pastoral life and labor, the core of which comprises the spirituality of the Exercises.

It would be a complete misunderstanding to conclude from this core message of the Book of the Exercises that the encounter with God happens primarily, indeed exclusively, in the Exercises. One could almost say that just the opposite is the case, and say it emphatically: The Exercises exist "only" to help persons, so that the encounter with God can occur "everywhere." With the Ignatian expression, "seeking and finding God in all things," we stand at the center of Ignatius's spirituality. Another important point is made with regard to the history of piety: In the person of Ignatius, it is as if we were clearly seeing God's — or actually the human person's — "breaking out" of "cloistered confinement" into the midst of the whole world. I am thinking here of the twentieth-century call for a "worldly piety," which was uttered and lived by so many believers, including spiritual adventurers like Pierre Teilhard de Chardin, S.J. All of them found an ally and "master of living" in sixteenth-century Ignatius.

Witnesses and testimonials tell us that contact with God happens in our own times, as well, and amid the darkest of situations. We meet one witness to the closeness of God, someone who knew of loneliness and dark nights, in the Jesuit Alfred Delp. Delp was arrested and sentenced to death during the Third Reich because he had contacts with the resistance movement

against Adolf Hitler. On November 17, 1944, just before the
proceedings which were to issue in his death sentence, he writes:

> One thing is preciously clear and tangible to me: the world
> is so full of God. This surges at us, as it were, out of all
> the pores. We get caught up in the beautiful hours and the
> bad. We do not live them through, live them to the point
> at which they stream forth from God. This goes for the
> beauty, as well as for all misery. In everything, God wants
> to celebrate encounter, and asks and wants the worshiping,
> loving answer. The challenge and the charge is only this: to
> make — or allow to develop — out of these insights and
> graces a permanent consciousness, and a permanent atti-
> tude. Then life becomes free, with the freedom we have so
> often sought. (Delp, 26)

Such a testimonial shows that Ignatius's words about seeking
and finding God "in all things," i.e., in all situations, are not
just "pious talk," but an authentic spiritual experience and a
guidepost.

God — in Surrender

In the fifteenth preliminary remark of the Exercises, already
cited, Ignatius speaks of the *anima devota,* the "devout soul,"
the devoted, dedicated, self-given, surrendered soul, which God
lovingly embraces. The word *devoción,* usually translated "devotion," plays a central role with Ignatius when it comes to a life
in the presence of God. "Devotion" for him does not mean an
odd little personal devotion, but the total surrender of a person.
Devotion means communication without holding back. Devotion means total attention and respect. In an earlier spiritual use
of language one spoke of "holocaust," of "total burnt offering,"
in the sense of a surrender that could go as far as surrendering
one's life in martyrdom. And spiritual experience knew enough
about life to be able to speak repeatedly about an "unbloody
martyrdom" as well.

What is meant by this devotion charged with self-giving? What meaning does "devotion" have for Ignatius? Anyone who in the past heard children's confessions knows something of the meaning of the word "devotion." When children went to confession, one could hear the pattern of their religious instruction: "I disobeyed my parents, I ate candy when my mother said not to, I wasn't devout at prayer." Not to be devout at prayer means: My thoughts were somewhere else instead of on my prayer; I thought in church about soccer games, or my toys, or school, or the like. I have chattered with my lips, but with my insides — my heart — I was somewhere else.

To be devout means to be totally attentive: as attentive as a child who is totally immersed in a game; as attentive as two lovers gazing at each other; as attentive as a scientist who looks in fascination at his discovery under the microscope; as attentive as a hiker observing a clearing in the woods, wondering whether an animal might appear.

The attention of "devotion" means not only an attention of the eyes, but also, and principally, an attention of the heart, the surrender of the whole heart. This attitude expresses Jesus' regard for an Old Testament verse about love for God: "You shall love the Lord your God with all your heart, and with all your soul, and with all your strength, and with all your mind..." (Luke 10:27; see also Deut. 6:4). The attitude of reverent, loving surrender is the basis of our relationship with God, of love of neighbor, and of love of oneself. It is the foundation of all of our speaking and all of our silence, of our doing and our "letting be." This becomes clear in a statement by Ignatius in a letter to his fellow Jesuit Francis Borgia. It has to do, among other things, with the question on how long one should pray. This was one of the questions that produced great conflict among the first generation of Jesuits. Some Jesuits came right out and said: one should actually be ashamed of how little time the Jesuits take for prayer, in comparison with other religious. In the letter under consideration, which addresses this question, it is pointed out that the important thing is a person's overall devo-

tion. Whether this devotion occurs in prayer or during study or
charitable activities, professional work, or political commitment
is a matter of secondary importance.

> It would be good if he considered that God makes use
> of persons not only when they pray. Were that the case,
> prayers would be too short if they lasted less than twenty-
> four hours a day, if that were possible. For the whole
> person must surrender to God as completely as possible.
> But as it happens, God occasionally makes use of other
> things more than prayer, to the point that he rejoices for
> their sake when one omits prayer, or rather, when prayer is
> shortened. Therefore it is in order to pray always, and not
> to slacken — but understanding it well, as the saints and
> doctors understand it. (BU, 290)

We could perhaps say that just as, for Paul in the First Letter
to the Corinthians (chap. 13), patient love, loving patience gives
everything else its value, so it is for Ignatius with surrender to
God. Only through love and patience do activity, speech, silence,
prayer, and work find their meaning. Devotion as surrender gives
and creates community with God.

Praying with All One's Might

The practice of Ignatian prayer is very rich and comprehensive.
It is best described in terms of the words Jesus uses when he
speaks of the heart of the Law, which is to love God with all
one's strength and all one's heart. The paraphrase "to pray with
all one's strength and all one's heart" summarizes Ignatian prayer
life. In Ignatian prayer, persons pray with their heads, in reflection, using comparisons, thinking through their lives before God.
They pray with their feelings, their emotions, their desires and
wants, with longing. They pray with all of their senses: with
the imagination, with inner images, bringing to life the biblical
events. They pray by interaction with the Bible, with literature.
They pray foremost with the "stuff of life": with encounters,

situations requiring decisions, moving experiences, joys, fears, hopes, memories, and the history of their own life. For each of the key words just cited, or for each power of the soul, examples of content and method could be found in the Book of the Exercises. Above all, the examination of conscience should help in learning to discover the "Gospel in life," the living Gospel.

Over the course of the history of piety a shift occurred that doesn't quite correspond to Ignatius's thinking. Some people who speak of the Ignatian way of prayer connect "Ignatian contemplation" almost exclusively with the contemplation of biblical scenes. Some readers fail to see in the Exercises helps for prayer of simplicity, prayer of quiet, prayer in which words are used little or not at all. Surely there is no missing the fact that in the Book of the Exercises, directives urging simplicity in prayer are not as emphatic as they are, say, in *The Cloud of Unknowing,* as in the writings of Teresa of Avila, as in the Jesus prayer from the *Righteous Tales of a Russian Pilgrim.* Ignatius is sometimes taken to be just a helper for "beginners." This is doubly inappropriate.

First, it's clear that it is *part of the totality of the human being* to pray "with all one's strength." It makes no sense for certain dimensions of the human being to be deliberately excluded from prayer. Obviously there are differences as to where to put the emphasis. Obviously it is possible that, over the course of years, someone's way of praying should change. For the encounter with Christ, an expressly Bible-oriented prayer — at least for a certain "formative period" — is unavoidable.

The other mistake with Ignatian prayer is to fail to see that it grows out of and returns to *a great simplicity.* "Simplicity" of prayer, which is so much spoken of today in connection with Eastern and Western meditation or contemplation, is found in Ignatius in manifold ways: it shows itself even in the oft-quoted instruction that it is not "an abundance of knowledge that feeds the soul, but the relishing of things from within." Better to chew over a text, a sentence, a word, ten times rather than move right on. In particular, the practice of immersing oneself in repeated contemplations expresses a tendency toward simplicity. For the five hours of meditation a day, Ignatius usually gives only two or three sets of "points." Everything else is a process of repetition, meant to instill simplification and deeper appreciation.

Again, in Ignatius's directives for the "three methods of prayer" in the Book of the Exercises we have the tendency to simplify. One should remain with a single word of one prayer as long as one finds it profitable. One may let words — one word, one name — move with the rhythm of one's breath, and so just "be there" in prayer. In the "Contemplation for Obtaining Love," the core of this "prayer posture," so to speak, is expressed with the words, "Take, Lord, and receive all my liberty, my memory, my understanding, and all my will — all that I have and possess. You, Lord, have given all that to me. I now give it back to you, O Lord. All of it is yours. Dispose of it according to your will. Give me your love and your grace, for that is enough for me" (GU, no. 234). This is a prayer uttered from the profoundest depths of the soul and in utmost simplicity and wholeness.

Perhaps the most helpful text as a lead to "simple prayer" is a passage in a letter of Ignatius to a Jesuit who was responsible for young confreres:

> [The students] should train themselves to seek the presence of God our Lord in all things, for example, in speaking, in walking, in seeing, in tasting, in hearing, in thinking — in everything they do. God's majesty is surely in all things, through his presence, through his work, and through his nature. To contemplate in such a way — by finding God our Lord in all things — is easier than if we were to seek to elevate ourselves to spiritual material of a more abstract kind, in which we can immerse ourselves only with difficulty. Too, this excellent exercise leads to great visitations of grace from the Lord, while at the same time preparing us for them. (GB, 206)

One may regret that Ignatius does not further explain what he means by "this excellent exercise" in more concrete terms.

But perhaps it is put in this way to make the point: Don't think much about it. Rather, be profoundly attentive to your breathing, and God's being will reveal itself to you. Be profoundly attentive to your looking, and God's being will reveal itself to you. Be profoundly attentive to your tasting, and God's being will reveal itself to you. Be profoundly attentive to your actions, and God's being will reveal itself to you. Be present with profound attention, and God's being will reveal itself to you — God whose name is "I am the I-am-present."

Ignatius's experience, like that of many who search for God, is that a single moment, in which the eyes of the heart open to God, can suffice for a whole lifetime. Then it is possible for God to be found in everything: in the sparkle of a dewdrop on a blade of grass, in a certain glow in a human face, in a desperate outcry to God, in a loving encounter and in a wrenching pain, in the deepest darkness and on the brightest day.

The most characteristic feature of Ignatian prayer is that contemplation is not only a way of praying, nor only a certain spiritual exercise for a given time, but a spiritual way of life. Living and praying and acting from the center of the heart are the expression of the simplicity of Ignatian prayer. The most important kind of praying existence for Ignatius was "walking in the presence of God."

Contemplation in Action: "So It'll Go Smoother"

Down through the centuries — one might almost say millennia — the question has been raised in Christian spirituality (and not only there) of the relationship between contemplation and action. Most often the discussion has been linked to the biblical scene of the listening Mary and the eagerly active Martha on the occasion of Jesus' visit. How are we to view the relationship of Mary and Martha, of contemplation and action? Ignatian spirituality has invented the dialectical formula *contemplativus in actione,* "contemplative in action." Or one could turn it around: *activus in contemplatione,* "active in contemplation."

> One must often think how the *vita activa* and *contemplativa* must go their way together.... Thus, a *vita activa superior* [a higher active life] ripens, in which action and contemplation have become one — a life that has the power to produce both everywhere, as corresponds to the greater service of our Lord. In a word: works of love, totally at one with God: That is perfect activity! (Nadal, 409)

The experience of a grandma and her little grandchild may possibly clarify the paradoxical ring of "contemplative action." Little Tanya was completely absorbed in playing with her toys. After half an hour she quietly approached her grandma, who was sitting in the same room, knitting. She walked over to Grandma, nudged her lightly with her elbow, saying, "So it'll go smoother," and returned to her toys, again becoming completely engrossed in her play. This story can serve as a parable and bring much to light about contemplative life-consciousness. The upper layer of little Tanya's consciousness and attention is concentrated entirely on her building blocks, dolls, and toy store. But there must be in her a kind of "background consciousness," with which she knows that Grandma is in the room. Apparently her half-conscious awareness of her connection to Grandma diminishes in a way that she can sense, as when one can become aware that the room temperature is dropping. And then the touch, the deliberate quick shift over to Grandma, becomes necessary "so it'll go smoother," and all's right with the world again.

This experience is an ideal commentary on what is called "ejaculatory prayer" in the spiritual tradition. The soul's quick look upward in the midst of activity or before the beginning of work is a "wake-up call" for the basic consciousness of a life in God's presence. All of the little girl's actions were borne by a basic contemplative consciousness, so that she could play and function in the presence of a loving person. If little Tanya — and this could happen too — had leaned against Grandma for half

an hour, that too would be a picture of activity in contemplation: active in the sense that the little girl could first have talked
about all she had done in her play. And afterward, after she has
prattled about up her experiences, if the little one quietly cuddles
up to Grandma, then her activities are no longer in the top stra-
tum of her consciousness, but they do continue to constitute the
life-space out of which she comes and to which she will return
in five minutes. This is a matter not of different worlds, but of a
singular "life-house," with different rooms, all interconnected.
Contemplative life-consciousness is the expression of a constant
communication with God. In the Acts of the Apostles, this basic
consciousness is described with a citation from a "heathen" poet:
"In him we live and move and have our being" (Acts 17:28).

Separation and Silence

There is no verbal communication without speech, but neither
is there communication without listening. Two loudspeakers
blaring at each other are not yet in conversation. This could
be extended: no listening without silence, no silence without
solitude, no togetherness without a capacity for solitude.

In the area of silence and listening, as well, Ignatius proves no
friend of technical terms, although it might have been especially
desirable here. He discusses, in the Book of the Exercises, for
only about a page, his view that the exercitant "will achieve
more progress the more he or she withdraws from all friends
and acquaintances and from all earthly concerns" (GU, no. 20).
Interestingly, Ignatius does not emphasize silence as such. An
atmosphere of quiet seems a given for him. He stresses other
matters, in which he principally sees the meaning and power of
quiet.

First, an act of "de-concerning" and liberation takes place. "A
person who is involved in public affairs or pressing occupations"
(GU, no. 19) can be totally caught up in a network of appointments and obligations. Changing one's house (see GU, no. 20)
can be a step into freedom, which Ignatius describes with dras-

tic pithiness, advising the reader "to make sure that you are not possessed by what you possess."

This turning away means at the same time a "turning toward," and a focusing of attention. Staking out one's own time and space implies a process like that of a married couple who, after years spent in rearing children and vacationing with them, finally once again go on vacation by themselves. This creates the external space in which their mutual encounter can happen again, in togetherness, in listening to each other, and this means in silence too, since one can listen only in silence.

The step into silence is also a step into solitude and into a capacity for making decisions. The outer situation helps to make it clearer what the individual person seeks and wants, and not what "polls," "majorities," and so on suggest. Thus Ignatius is familiar, during the important business of electing a superior general, with both times for "buzzing" (*murmuratio*) and times of complete silence, where one must make decisions in the sight of God, as it were in the face of death. Solitude and silence are very closely connected.

The decision for silence is also a decision for "actuality," for what, deep down, I really desire. Often, throughout the "daily grind," a person's deepest longings are covered over and repressed. According to Ignatius, in silence "we enjoy a freer use of our natural faculties for seeking diligently what we so ardently desire" (GU, no. 20).

Furthermore, a "yes" to separation and silence aims at a receptivity for emptiness and poverty. The fruitfulness of such an existence, which holds itself open to God like a vessel, is affirmed by Ignatius with the words, "Every day we come to know more how true the phrase is, '. . . As having nothing, and yet possessing everything' (2 Cor. 6:10) — everything, I say, that God has promised those who seek first his kingdom and its righteousness" (GB, no. 92; see Luke 12:31 and par.).

Put simply, silent listening means: "The more we keep ourselves alone and secluded, the more fit do we make ourselves to approach and attain to our Creator and Lord" (GU, no. 20).

Dying, Which Leads to Life:
Free of Me and Open to You

In emptying oneself, one can leave room within for the other. One who knows how to be silent can hear the other. To become empty is a little akin to dying, with the dying of that self that would spread out everywhere and keep all the room for itself. Only the demise of this "territorial I" can make space for encounter and the joy of encounter. A remark of Ignatius bears on this joyfulness that comes of making room: "When one has gone out of oneself and has entered into one's Creator and Lord, always beholding, always sensing, always rejoicing in how our eternal Good inhabits all creation, giving it life and sustenance through his ever-present immensity — therein, as I see it, lies the very highest happiness" (GB, 58).

Books promising a successful life and ways to obtain happiness are a booming business nowadays. Ignatius's answer to the question of happiness is: Happy is the one who lives totally in communication and community with God. Joyful is the one who, in everything and with everything, is totally devoted to God. Happy is the one who does not just circle around the self, but totally surrenders to the "God in all persons and things."

Among these statements, one most particularly deserving of attention is: "When one has gone out of oneself and has entered into one's Creator and Lord. . . . " That is in order to arrive at true happiness in life, one needs to move out, embark on an exodus, move to a liberation from the little "I" that knows only itself, that feels its independence threatened by any intensive devotion to a relationship, and therefore refuses and blocks encounter. This little "ego-I" must die; otherwise it remains alone, precisely as we read in the Gospel of John: "Unless a grain of wheat falls into the earth and dies, it remains just a single grain" (John 12:24). If the grain of wheat wishes to keep itself, it remains sterile, with the mass of another thousands upon thousands of grains in a granary, where it cannot germinate, open up and bear fruit. Only if the grain of wheat falls to the ground and dies and sprouts, will new life develop — the living, organic, fruitful entity of the ear of wheat.

Against this background, a short comment by Ignatius becomes understandable. Once several Jesuits were having an admiring conversation about a confrere. One said, in a reverential tone, "Now, there is a man of prayer." Ignatius reacted with the comment, "Yes, he is a man of mortification." That is, he is a person who has been delivered from his little "I" for the encounter with God and the world — a person who has gone out of himself, has wrenched free from the compulsive fear of losing himself, a person who moves toward others, who surrenders himself, who loves. Only one who is able to be "free of me" in this sense, is "open to you." Looked at in this way, love is always the true ec-stasy, the true ex-odus, the true going-out-of-oneself. And with that, love is also true happiness.

Little Tanya expressed it well: "Some people are so big and loud they fill up the whole room and don't leave any room for me." By contrast, we could say that some people are so "free of me" that there is a great deal of room for a "you," and for encounter.

God's Language Is Reality

Communication is a two-sided process. But often enough, specifically in the matter of communication in prayer, the question is asked: Is not this "conversation" really one-sided? The way a human being feels and speaks when pleading, asking, thanking, praising is open to the experience and grasp of the one who prays. But how does God answer? By keeping silent? Does not prayer often enough seem like a telephone conversation where we can say everything into the mouthpiece but never hear an answer through the receiver?

Jesuit superior general Peter-Hans Kolvenbach responds to this question in a remarkable article, "Meister Ignatius, Mann des Wortes" (Master Ignatius, man of the word), published in 1994. In it he declares that, in prayer, "Ignatius expects . . . no word in answer." But Ignatius does expect us to perceive an answer from God through inner stirrings and motions. The entire "discernment of spirits" presupposes that God's Spirit makes itself known through motions that move us in the direction of more faith, hope, and love. One's own inner thoughts, tears, outward signs, feelings of consolation and peace, sense of "agreeableness" — all of these nonverbal happenings point toward a manner in which God answers the one praying. The art of the "discernment of spirits" means practice in hearing and perceiving the language of God.

Paul is a witness to the fact that God speaks this way in us: "We do not know how to pray as we ought, but that very spirit intercedes with sighs too deep for words" (Rom. 8:26). In Second Corinthians, the sacred writer puts it quite paradoxically: God's Spirit speaks to us in unspeakable words (cf. 2 Cor. 12:4).

One could say this, as well: God's language is reality. That is made clearest in the creation story. God speaks, and reality happens. God's speaking is creative. When God speaks, what appears is not a new book, but a new reality. Anyone wishing to discover and understand God's language must learn to decipher the language of reality, the language of life.

Guiding Light of Longing

The motion within a person that speaks most often and most clearly of God is perhaps longing. There is a story of the student who asked his rabbi, "Rabbi, where is God?" And the rabbi answered, "Tell me where God is not!" Ignatius's answer could run: God is where you seek God. Or to put it differently: God is with you when you seek God. God is in your inmost longing.

The clearest indication that God is closest to us in the language of longing probably lies in the fact that Ignatius encourages us to notice, before each meditation, the last, profoundest longing of our heart, as well as our altogether concrete wishes for this particular moment of prayer, and find words for them. This may remind us of Jesus' repeated question, "What do you wish?

What do you want me to do for you?" This question points, shall we say, to the path to be traced to the source of inner life and longing. There too lies the power for healing, holiness, and transformation.

There is a whole series of testimonials and thoughts in spiritual tradition confirming the fundamental role of longing. The best known is probably that of Augustine: "You have made us for yourself, O Lord, and our heart is restless till it rests in you!" With Augustine too we find almost the diametrical correlative: "God's desire is the human being." God and the human being meet in longing. And the question, often mentioned earlier, of what is meant by constant prayer is answered in this way by Augustine: "Faith, hope, love are a constant prayer of longing. Yet at certain times and hours we pray with words as well, and our longing becomes all the stronger."

Had Ignatius been party to the dialogue between religion and atheism, he certainly would have sought to propound the true longing of human existence, of the human heart. Godlessness would seem to him a betrayal of our longing. And he probably would have agreed with religious philosopher Franz von Baader's comparison: As thirst proves the existence of water, so God's existence shows itself in the longing for God. Nor would Ignatius have brooked arbitrary reinterpretations, such as: There are those who say that, "when all is said and done," longing for God only means longing for a fulfilled life, for a finding of oneself, for a happy encounter with another person. No, we can say that the longing for God is human beings' longing for themselves, in the sense that their longing for themselves is a yearning for their innermost core, and that is God. The longing for oneself finds its fulfillment in the fulfillment of the longing for God.

Communion and Communication

A famous painting by Rubens, like many other pictures of Ignatius, shows him in a chasuble. The chasuble belongs to the core realm of Ignatius's spiritual life. Church history shows that, wherever Jesuits worked, celebration of the Mass was widespread, and, above all, the invitation was issued to receive Holy Communion often. While the general custom was to receive Communion only once a year, or a few times a year, Ignatius and his group encouraged its frequent reception. This suggests the value of a brief look at the Mass as the ritual-sacramental expression of love, of communion, and of the communication of life.

Basic Eucharistic Attitudes — for Communication

Anyone closely examining the structure of the Mass, its individual parts and key prayers, can discover that the basic actions of the Eucharist express what it is that love, encounter, and genuine communication live on:

- Love lives on *respect for mystery*, as we see in the phrase, "the mystery of faith," the word of the community that it uses for its response after the Consecration.

- Love lives on the unity of body, mind, and spirit. This shows itself in the Eucharist in physical gestures, music, words, and images.

- Love lives on praise and thanksgiving. The word "Eucharist" ("praise and thanksgiving") points to this, as do various prayers of praise and thanks.

- Love lives on conversion and reconciliation, as the ritual of penance and forgiveness at the beginning of each Holy Mass reminds us, together with a series of prayers during the Mass.

- Love lives on hearing and answering the Gospel of Jesus. The entire celebration of the Eucharist is a back-and-forth of hearing, internalizing, and responding.

- Love lives on receiving and giving, as comes to tangible expression in the preparation of the gifts and the symbol-laden ritual of receiving and offering the gifts of bread and wine, those elements expressing the union of God's creative generosity and human toil.

- Love lives on transformation, on dying and resurrection. This is the pinnacle of the eucharistic event.

- Love lives on intimate encounter, on becoming one, on communion; is there a more intimate sign of union than "incorporation"?

- Finally, love lives on mission: "Go forth!" says the celebrant at the end of Mass, not "Please, stay here all together."

These basic elements of the Eucharist can be spelled out and made concrete in terms of the encounter among persons. On the subject of communication, they tell us that it matters whether you encounter one another with body, mind, and soul, holistically — whether you honor the other as a mystery, whether you are open to crisis and reconciliation, whether you allow yourself space for listening and talking, whether you mutually give and receive, whether you are open for transformation, whether you become involved with real "communion," whether you set out again and again with an eye to the world. When these eucharistic foundations of communication are disregarded, communication suffers — falls short of love and fulfillment.

"You Are What You Eat"

What matters to Ignatius with regard to the Eucharist is becoming one with Christ, God's love in human form. In the Eucharist, the saying, "You are what you eat," finds realization. Human beings live on the bread of human labor, and they live on the Bread of God, on God. There is probably no more telling symbol of unity than the taking of nourishment. By eating, we become one with what is eaten. We assimilate the nourishment and thereby sustain our life. Nourishment is not only a question of pleasure;

it is a question of life and death. This was Israel's acute experience in all the years of their journey through the desert, the journey of the miraculous feeding with manna, the "bread from heaven" and water from the rocks.

For the communities of Jesus' disciples, the celebration of the Last Supper became a central faith experience of union with Christ. "You are my nourishment, you are all my life, O Jesus!" says a Communion song in a hymnal used at Mass. We receive life from one another. We receive life from God. This occurs with the faithful in Holy Communion, and Communion makes it visible.

It would be a misunderstanding to regard this view of faith only "ritualistically." For Ignatius, the liturgical event was directly tied up with his life. This became clearly visible through the fact (among other things) that he often placed his questions as to decisions and his reflections in the form of written notes on the altar. Thus, he wanted to test, as it were, whether his endeavors and plans would stand up to the event of the Eucharist. How does such and such look when I consider it in relation to the living, suffering, and victorious love of God?

"Communion through Action" (Teilhard de Chardin) and Suffering

In the twentieth century Teilhard de Chardin, S.J., became a unique prophetic figure. In deep faith, he celebrated his "Mass upon the World," in which the entire cosmos and all of human history turn into the process of communion. For Teilhard existential communion with God takes place primarily in action, exploration, and work.

> In action, I first unite with the creative power of God. I fall in line with it. I become not only its tool, but its living extension. And because nothing is more intrinsic to a being than the will of God, I merge in a certain way, through my heart, with the heart of God. This is a permanent contact, as I am always active....

In this communion, the soul neither stands still in order to bathe in its delights, nor does it lose sight of the material aim of its activity. Does it not wed itself to a creative endeavor?...

Each instance of growth that I bestow on myself or on things is reflected in an increase in my capacity to love and in a progress toward Christ's blessed inhabitation of the universe. Our work appears to us above all as a means of earning our daily bread. Yet its definitive power is far superior: through it we complete in ourselves the personal element of the divine unification; and through it we enlarge, in a certain sense, in regard to ourselves, the divine element of that unification, our Lord Jesus Christ. (Teilhard de Chardin, 46–47)

While Teilhard primarily expresses the active side of communion (although he knew much, from his own experience and suffering, about "passivity" and pain), it is Paul Claudel who brings the passive side of communion especially to light. His play *The Silken Shoe* opens with a scene which makes it clear that the faithful celebrate the Eucharist with their whole life, and especially by their surrender to God. In the introductory scene, a Jesuit priest whom pirates have bound to the mast of a deserted and sinking ship, speaks: "I have given myself to you, O God, and now the day of rest and release has come. Now I can surrender to my bonds. And now, behold, the final prayer of that Mass commences that I celebrate with the bread of my own existence."

When Ignatius came to die, he would have liked to have the papal blessing. But the Secretary neglected to pursue his wish promptly because of a number of important letters still unattended to. So Ignatius died during the night without the requested comfort. The last that the brother infirmarian heard through the door was a repeated "Ay, Dios! Ay, Dios!" "O God! O God!" He died, one wrote at the time, "a death like anyone else's." Alone, but at one with the One from whom he had drawn his life.

Chapter 11

God Is Encounter

The Triune God in the Mirror of I–You–We

We all know the saying, "Tell me what company you keep and I'll tell you who you are." The person with whom I like to "hang around," the person with whom I sympathize, whose living habits or interests I share — all of these say something essential about myself. To put it more flatly: Encounters rub off on you. One could also say: Tell me what God you believe in, and I'll tell you who you are. Tell me how you behave when you're with God, and I'll tell you how you encounter people. In what God do I believe? In what God do Christians believe? How do we "behave" with God? Who are we? We are Christians. How do Christians meet each other, and others?

God Is Relation

For years now, we have heard a great deal concerning the "dialogue of the religions," and that dialogue — thank God — indeed manages to survive and flourish, great though the obstacles be. Consider the invitation of various religious communities by John Paul II to a service of gratitude in Assisi, Francis's home city. The point of departure for the conversation of the religious communities with one another is often the question concerning common elements and differences in their conception of God. When the meaningful and necessary question is posed as to the differences in the elements of their faith, then, usually very early, we hear: the Christian idea of God is "Trinitarian." And it is said that this is a very important difference, if not the decisive one, vis-à-vis other ideas of God. This is how the Christian partners to the conversation see things, and most often the "others" too.

What is the meaning of the statement that God is "threefold" or "triune" or "Trinitarian"? How are these words of faith to be understood? Not infrequently, the answer comes that they refer to a mystery of faith that transcends all human conceiving. And not infrequently we hear in this connection a very eloquent story from the life of Augustine. One day Augustine was in Ostia, the Roman seaport, strolling on the beach. He was deep in thought, seeking to get to the bottom of the threefold God. Suddenly he saw a little child, who was pouring water from the sea into a little hole in the sand. When asked what he was doing, the child answered, "I'm pouring the sea into this hole." With benign amusement, Augustine responded: "But child, look at that great, endless sea. You can't get that into your little hole in the sand!" To which the child responded to the great theologian: "Nor can you grasp the mystery of the triune God with your understanding."

This fable is as beautiful as it is simple and impressive. It ought to stand at beginning and end of all discourse upon the mysteries of faith and God. But certain questions remain: What is meant by the message of the Trinitarian faith? What does the Gospel tell us about the reality, the life, of the threefold God? And finally, what does this message have to do with the question of communication, and with the communicative dimension of Ignatian spirituality?

Perhaps we discern something of the connection between communication and belief in the Trinitarian God when we hear certain basic statements intended to convey who and "how" God is. God is love. God is life. God is relation, as traditional theology teaches of the being, the life of God understood in terms of a Trinity. God *is* relation, we hear. In other words, God's being, God's essence is *communio* of love, a community of love. God's being is a being-itself in a communicating of self. The much-cited expression of Jewish philosopher of religion Martin

Buber — "All real life is encounter" — is valid in a basic way for the life of God. God is life, God is relation, God is encounter.

Divine Triad

Ignatius of Loyola grew up in this faith in the Trinitarian God. In particular, his mystical diary shows that this faith for him was not only the repetition of a tenet of faith that is not, and cannot be, understood, but also a dogma that stamped his spiritual experiences to their depths. We have vague indications from his companions that he himself worked on a brief manuscript about the mystery of the Trinity. Unfortunately, this writing, if Ignatius actually did produce it, was not preserved and never published. If Ignatius had thought its publication meaningful, it certainly would have taken place. Perhaps he spared us a disappointment, or spared himself the title of Doctor of the Church. Be all this as it may, we remain dependent on the few traces in his terse remarks and on his spiritual diary.

On this quest, we have first a documented trace of images and likenesses. Once, Ignatius writes, he had a vision of the Trinity in the form of three keys on an organ. He does not expand on this image, but perhaps we may interpret it in the following sense. The mystery of the divine love is like a three-note chord. God is one ringing, vibrating chord of divine music. God is not only an individual note, but like a musical triad. God's oneness is to be one-in-fullness, one sound made up of different notes.

For Ignatius, this intuition is neither a play of theological fantasy nor the abstract numbers game of a mathematical theology. For him this was a "fact," a "thing," of deepest emotion, of mysticism, of ecstasy, of living faith. His companions report that the very sight of three blossoms, three doves, or another triple object was enough to cast Ignatius into a paroxysm of profound Trinitarian belief. Any symbol of the Trinitarian love had the effect of suffusing his deepest inner life with God.

This intimate link with the divine mystery in no way means, however, that Ignatius thought he had "figured out" God, that "vision" as opposed to "faith" had been given to him in the sense that he saw through the mystery of the divine life. In his mystical diary itself we find observations that show that he had a difficult time with a believing grasp of the Trinitarian mystery. He speaks of experiencing a "knot," which was undone only after many quests and much reflection: "That this knot, or whatever it is, should be undone, seemed to me so important that I could not leave off speaking and saying from within me: Who are you (Ignatius)? Where are you headed? Why such things (these great revelations)? Where do they come from? Yes, how can you have deserved all this? And so on" (GT, 168).

Ignatius's Trinitarian mysticism, his view of the Trinity, is an extensive, complicated theme. It is certain that Ignatius lived in extraordinary ways on the mystery of the Trinitarian God. And it is certain that, only after a long journey, this mystery revealed itself to him ever more profoundly.

Biblical Starting Point

The biblical approach to an understanding of the Christian Trinitarian faith in God can only be sketchy. The growth of the Christian belief in God was marked by four basic spiritual experiences of the first Christian generation: the experience of God, the experience of Jesus, the experience of the Holy Spirit, and the reciprocal relationship of these foundational spiritual experiences.

1. For most of the first Christians, *trust in Yahweh,* the God of the Jewish people, was the foundation of their religious devotion. They lived in and on the covenant of God with the chosen people, Israel. They recalled Yahweh's deeds in history. In the Psalms, they cried out to their faraway and near God, their active and hidden God. They praised God, they relied on God. They discerned God's nearness in trembling vision. Through their encounter with Jesus, and Jesus' relationship with the "Father," the "Daddy God," many of them found themselves using an almost unspeakably tender, trusting tone in their relationship with God.

2. A second foundational experience of the first Christians was their *encounter with Jesus*. Through Jesus, whom they soon called Christ, God had come near, amid their very life, more than anything or anyone else. Their salvation, their hopes, all that they awaited from God, came in the encounter with Jesus in their life. The more than one hundred names and images of God in the New Testament — especially in the Epistles — are a testimonial to a kind of "relationship explosion." The first Christians neither could nor wanted to speak of God, of salvation, of redemption, without Jesus, whom they called Messiah, Christ. The response of the "Johannine Christ" to the petition to be allowed to see the Father, is an expression of this experience of Jesus' importance and oneness with "the Father": "Who sees me, sees the Father!"

3. A third basic experience, not to be overlooked, was added in the *experience of the Holy Spirit*. The first Christian communities were Holy Spirit communities and through the Spirit-God and that Spirit's charisms, through the gifts of the Holy Spirit, grew to be a "Temple of living stones." Baptism in the Holy Spirit ranked as one of the most important signs of identity and marks of distinction vis-à-vis other modes of faith. The Spirit of God filled them as the gift promised by Jesus. The individual's life drew its strength from life "in the Holy Spirit." In experiences of the Spirit, they perceived the love of God poured forth "into their hearts." In the Holy Spirit, they dared — even Peter, who had, the New Testament tells us, said "Never" to the radically new four times — to take the step beyond the Jewish law. In this Spirit, they experienced "the Lord" as near to them. Indeed, the Lord *is* the Spirit, and whoever denies the Lord, denies the true Spirit.

From all of this, it became increasingly clear to the first Christians that — if they wished the reality of God to come to expression completely in their life — they must always speak of the Father, the Son, and the Sprit. These three distinct foundational experiences flowed together *into a single "spiritual faith-movement"* — perhaps we could dub it the "dance of faith." In it, the distinction and interior "oscillation" of persons was perceived and safeguarded. Baptism, the "public" entry into the community of Christians, is conferred "in the name of the Father, and of the Son, and of the Holy Spirit." This is the primitive Christian, Trinitarian, "abbreviated creed."

Human beings have the capacity to give systematic expression and form to their experiences and their belief in order to pass them on and communicate them. Such attempts have always been made with respect to faith in God and the experience of God. In Yahweh, the early Christians experienced the "God above us," in Christ the "God facing us," and in the Holy Spirit the "God within us." With this and all systematizations, and with the attempt to understand one's own faith on a deeper level, it must never be forgotten that the basis of Christian faith has always been anchored in three foundational spiritual experiences of faith on the part of the first Christian generations. From these experiences, there flowed a never-ending, dynamic movement of Christian faith in God: the notion that (1) God is relationship and love, (2) God is loving, reciprocal in-spiration, and (3) life is the dance of the interpenetration of unity and distinction. God is *Communio* — a declaration that is not made for the sake of a theological system or the title of a book, but is an attempt to take Christian faith seriously and to encase it in words.

In the continuation and depiction of the biblical starting point of the Trinitarian teaching in the course of church history, there is much that is acceptable and unacceptable — beautiful and strange thought-constructions, images, symbols, and likenesses, calculated to express the Trinitarian "mystery of faith." They extend from the triangle to magnificent icons, from monstrous pictures forbidden by the church to the wonderful fresco of the Trinity in a Bavarian church in Urschalling, in which, in the countenance of the Holy Spirit, a woman's face can be seen. Human faculties such as understanding, will, and memory, and the human family of father, mother, and child have served as helps to an understanding of the incomprehensible mystery of God. In what follows, we shall explain three basic human words as a primordial image of the Trinitarian phenomenon: the words "I," "thou," and "we." As a concrete likeness, an experiential human reality, they are especially suitable for the purpose of clarifying encounter, the process of relationship, personal interiority and distinction, *Communio* and Communication. In so doing, we can discern a special kinship of the "I" with the paternal/ maternal, of the "thou" with the filial quality, and of the "we" with the Holy Spirit, in the mystery of God.

"Being I" as the Expression of the Parental Mystery of God

The little word "I" is one of the most used words in our life, in our speech: "I think, I'd like, I'm coming...." A great deal is hidden in our saying "I," and still more in our being "I." Three elements should be especially emphasized here: Being "I" implies *mystery, creativity,* and *authority.* These three dimensions point in a special way to the mystery of God as Father and Mother. This will first be briefly demonstrated from the Bible and then looked at as it corresponds to human communication.

God, a Mystery: "I Am Who I Am"

One of the most impressive passages in the Old Testament, in the Testament of First Beginnings, is the revelation of God's name to Moses. Out of the strange apparition of the burning bush that did not burn up, Moses receives an answer to his question in the form of the name of God: "I am the I-am-here." There are many attempts at a translation of this strange name: "I am the I-am," "I shall be who I shall be," "I am where you are" (Martin Buber), "I am [the one] who is with you." One thing is common to all of these translations: They evince the mysteriousness of God more than they explain it. Thus I Am means to be a mystery. God is so much of a mystery, a mystery that calls for reverence, that Jews do not directly pronounce the Name of God, but paraphrase it instead as: "The Most High, the Lord...." So much is God a mystery that there is a strict prohibition against making images of God.

That God is a mystery, and is revealed in and as a mystery, is shown in Jesus, as well. A clear testimonial to this is the so-called "Messianic secret." It is most striking in Mark. It sounds almost grotesque when Jesus orders those he has healed, the disciples, and the people not to speak of him and not to make him the Messiah. Why should a person who can see again not speak of the one who has bestowed this gift?

Who is Jesus? In Matthew, he is called "Immanuel," an Old Testament reference: "God with us." And we hear the echo of God's mysterious name, "I am the I-am-here." As we have pointed out, over one hundred names, images, and titles of Jesus are to be found in the New Testament, and not only familiar ones like "the Christ," "Son of Man," "Son of David." And yet it remains true: "One stands in your midst whom you know not." Thus, in Jesus, too, is reflected the mysteriousness of the I-mystery of God.

God: Wellspring of All Creativity

Just as God is a mystery as Father, so God is also the wellspring of all creativity, all creative action. God is might, strength, creative power. God's word is never mentioned casually: it is, and makes, reality. Nowhere does this appear as clearly as in the account of creation: God speaks, and light and life arise, plants spring up, beasts find their place at the heart of nature. God's creative word gives humans existence and names, a face and a community. In particular, the process of blessing — as a noun and as a verb — moves along this line, and extends it. To be blessed means: life and riches, land and bread, children and relatives, recognition and justice.

God's mighty gift of life is shown not only in this rather agricultural vision, but also in the divine historical initiatives. God not only sets the scene, so to speak, and positions persons there, but personally functions, mysteriously, as actually

present, and as co-player, in the process of the history of humanity. Providence and initiative, the making of a covenant with the
chosen people, and the word uttered "through the mouth of the
prophets" are all historical expressions and apparitions of God's
creative reality, God's "working."

In the theology of the New Testament, in whose view the brilliance of the Father is reflected in the visage of Christ, Christ and
the mystery of creation are bound together in utter intimacy. In
the Gospel of John, he is the eternal Logos, who was at the beginning of everything and in and through whom everything has
been created (see John 1:1–17). "He is the image of the invisible
God, the firstborn of all creation; for in him all things in heaven
and on earth were created" (Col. 1:15–16).

As Savior and Redeemer of creation, as well, a creation that
seems definitively threatened by sin and death and surely doomed
to annihilation, Jesus is shown as God's hand, as Yahweh's
mouth and finger. Out of the darkness arises the new creation.
When Jesus calls disciples to follow him, he is "creating" disciples for himself. Exegetes indicate that in the phrase, "He *made*
them his disciples," the same word is used as in the creation account. Not only does Jesus call the disciples to himself, but he
"creates" his disciples. In the mystery of his death and resurrection, finally, love demonstrates its creative might in its victory
over the destructive powers of sin and death.

God Is Life-Dispensing Authority

Intimately bound up with creativity is the authority of the
motherly/fatherly mystery of God. This may actually sound
astonishing in our time, since, at least beginning with the En-
lightenment and continuing in the anti-authoritarian student
revolutions, authority is associated rather with the concept of
"impeding life" than with that of "dispensing life." Nevertheless,
the earliest sense of "authority" has its origin in the mystery of
life. This is clearest with parents' procreation and "education"
or rearing of their children. Presumably it was in the light of this

phenomenon that the word "authority" (compare "author") was invented and coined. In Latin, the root *augere* means cause to grow, multiply, increase. In his sense, authority is everything and every person who dispenses life out of the power and love of his or her being, who takes loving care of life, who makes life live.

Yahweh is the God of life, who bestows life through the power and might of the divine word. Even God's commandments and prohibitions are understood at bottom as words of life. The Ten Commandments are not ten life-denying regulations and strangulations, but are words of life. "Deca-logue" comes from the Greek and means "ten words." The sacred writers of the Old Testament testify to their experience in another passage when they say: Once spoken forth, Yahweh's word does not return without having succeeded. It effects what it intends: the life of persons.

The same power and authority is reflected in Jesus' being and word: "It was said of old,... but I say to you...!" Behind such words, and behind Jesus' activity, which matches his words, stand power, might, and authority. Therefore the people say of him: He speaks as one who has authority, not as the doctors of the law and the Pharisees. With Jesus, too, it is clear that he places might and authority in the service of life. Therefore he enjoins his disciples: "The lords of this world enslave their subjects. It is not to be that way with you!" Your authority shall be authority that bestows life and guards life.

I-Being and I-Saying in Communication

Jesus says of himself, "Who sees me, sees the Father." We read in the creation account of the book of Genesis that we human beings have been created in the likeness of God: "In the image of God he created them." This also means that human beings are called to live their I-being and therein to reflect God's I-being. In this sense, the acceptance of one's own existence is the first act of divine worship. Romano Guardini once put this in a striking way: "Acceptance of oneself" is the prerequisite for all further growth and activity. The first religious act occurs not in "self-denial," but in the acceptance of self out of gratitude. In the measure that we accept our true, godlike I-being, in that same measure we live the mysteriousness, the creativity, and the authority of human existence.

Attending to the Mystery of the I-Being

The human being: a mystery. Persons not completely corrupted by purely rationalistic, purely secular, thinking can experience in themselves that they are mystery for themselves and others. *Individuum est ineffabile,* the individual is inexpressible, as an old formulation goes. Nor is this a matter of philosophical propositions; instead, it is a matter of being human and of human encounter. Those who lose sight of the mystery of their person stand in danger — as Karl Rahner puts it — of evolving backward into brute beasts.

Human communication is the act of that person alone who observes and reveres the otherness of the thou, the "you." Human encounter is the act of one who fashions "no image of the other." For the relationship of person to person, as well, the biblical prohibition of images holds. True, we constantly make ourselves pictures of ourselves and of others. The crucial question, however, is whether these images — to borrow a concept from photography — are fixed and thereby inalterable (whether we clamp the other once and for all into a picture frame), or whether we — in biblical imagery this time — "judge as if we judged not."

The Creative Creature

God as potter and creation as clay: a favorite biblical image. But God's creation is creative, too. God has not reserved this to the divinity alone. The human being, too, may and should be creative, and thereby be an image of the creative God. Wherever someone begins something, wherever someone takes the initiative, wherever someone dreams "concrete utopias," wherever someone entertains "creative pauses," there is reverence of God as Creator.

I remember a religious sister, middle-aged, who reminded me of a nervous, startled chicken. She told me a story. "Father, if you only knew how I was earlier, till my sixteenth year: young, fresh, strong, intelligent. That changed the day I got high honors in school and came home with the news. And all I heard was, 'Just don't get stuck up!' Later, in the order, I often heard, when I had some especially good success, 'Just don't become proud, Sister!' And now I don't trust myself any more!"

I do not know what tone this woman used when recounting her school achievements at home. I do not know how simply and naturally she behaved on the occasion of her successes in the order. But one thing is certain: there is such a thing as insensitive brain-washing, there is such a thing as the internalization of a false modesty, there is a false humility, there is the biblical parable of the talent that the servant buries instead of working and living with it. And there is such a thing as a "yes" to oneself, which at the same time is reverence to God and says, to divine gifts, not "No, thank you," but "Yes, please."

To Be Authority for One Another

One of the worst accusations, and one that many people least like to hear, is that somebody is "authoritarian." Anyone having to suffer under the authoritarian behavior of others knows how wounding, how uncomfortable, how life-restricting unjust or abused authority can be. This shoe one can do without. But is this not throwing out the baby with the bath water, as so often in human life? Does authority not also mean: accepting responsibility, drawing salutary lines, answering for someone or something, to be responsible for...? Does fear of being authority and observing the injunctions of authority produce also the complaint of the "orphan society"? And do we not build false authorities this way, by entrenching ourselves behind authorities instead of ourselves assuming authority, properly understood, in our place? Does not the proliferation of laws, documents, instructions, and so on constantly grow because everything must always be exactly safeguarded, and there is too little personal trust, or too little of it is invested in others? Is not the reason for all the anonymity and namelessness that too many people are afraid to "lend their names to . . . "?

More questions: Isn't Being-I, deep down, essentially about being an authority and concretely expressing that? Those who see themselves as a real "I," and who have a "strong ego," may also think of themselves as an authority. They do not hide behind other persons' opinions, but are ready to say yes and no. With Jesus' words, "Let your yes be a yes and your no be a no," one can discern a great deal of the origin and essence of authority, which he attributed to our words and behavior and expected of them.

Thou-Being as an Expression of the Filial Mystery of God

In the eternal Son in God, we behold the thou-mystery of God. The Son is the "Thou" in God, God's own self-image.

As all human beings are an I, so are they also a thou. Persons are a thou when they face themselves — for example, in talking to themselves — and a thou for others. Thou-being is one of the most precious elements of life. To offer someone one's thou in the profound sense not only serves to simplify a conversation, but can be an expression or the beginning of authentic encounter.

Also in thou-being and thou-saying there are many hues and realities. The capacity to *hear* and to *receive*, to *listen* and to *give oneself* or *step beyond oneself* certainly belong to its inner core.

"Hear, O Israel": Hearing and Receiving

The Jews' daily morning prayer begins with the cry, "Hear, O Israel!" With these words, the prophets jolt Israel to attention. With this call, Yahweh seeks to render his people attentive to the divine being and word. Hearing — the basis of all communication.

When Pope John Paul II, on the occasion of a visit to the German College in Rome, was asked by a seminarian what he had to say of obedience, the answer, perhaps with a little bit of side-stepping, but altogether correct as well, was: "Obedience comes from listening. Obedience begins with listening and hearing."

Hearing, listening, and capacity for the "thou" are very closely intertwined. Wherever there is no listening, there can be no communication, no hearing, and no obedience. Jesus once expressed his great sorrow regarding the people with a saying from the Old Testament: "They have ears and hear not!" He himself, the perfect image of God, lives by hearing and listening: "My bread is to do the will of him who sent me." As Jesus listens to the father's word, so he listens to human beings as well. "What would you have me do for you?" One could almost ask in puzzlement, why Jesus asks such a "dumb question." After all, it is clear that a sick person wants to be cured. And yet it seems important that, through Jesus' question, he makes appeal to the freedom of the sick person, to that person's inmost will, and thus provokes a deeper desire.

The intensity of the transition from Jesus' listening to his obedience is shown most of all in his agony on the Mount of Olives. Here he expresses his misery, his imploring anguish, but also his readiness for the obedience of love: "Father, if it be possible, let this cup pass; yet not my will, but yours be done."

"Take and Receive": Obedience and Gift of Self

Ignatius's famous "Suscipe" prayer in the Exercises begins with the words: "Take and receive, O Lord, all my liberty...." This surrender is an answer to all of the gifts that God has given — indeed, including God's very self. In a receiving-and-hearing acceptance occurs the transition to a responsive surrender. Those who receive in hearing can give themselves in answer. Those who listen can obey in trust and make a gift of themselves in obedience. In the Old Testament, God meets us again and again as the one who listens to the petitions of his people and bestows life and blessing upon them. God is a listening God and cries out in frustration, as Israel utters the reproach that God does not listen, "How can the one who has created the ear not be able to hear?" Even in the account of creation, God makes a self-gift to creation, and the covenant with the people of God stands for the limitless divine readiness to take part in the history of that people — or as Jesus promised his disciples: "I am with you to the end of the world."

In the Son, in Jesus, God's self-gift is so apparent that Paul asks, "Will he not with him also give us everything else?" (Rom. 8:32). In the Gospel of John, we read the believing certitude: "For God so loved the world that he gave his only Son, so that everyone who believes in him may not perish but may have eternal life" (John 3:16). Ignatius expresses this experience of faith in his directions for the Contemplation to Obtain Love:

> I will call into my memory the gifts I have received — my creation, redemption, and other gifts particular to myself. I will ponder with deep affection how much God our Lord has done for me, and how much he has given me of what he possesses, and consequently how he, the same Lord, desires to give me even his very self, in accordance with his divine design. (GU, no. 234)

With regard to Jesus' being and life, theologians sometimes talk about a "pro-existence," that is, of a life as "existing-for." This existence-for gives direction and meaning to Jesus and his life. He lives in his mission, that is, he comes from the Father and goes to human beings. He comes from encounter and goes to encounter.

Being-Thou and Saying-Thou in Communication

The mystery of the divine Trinity is no sheer theological speculation. In being-thou, in saying-thou, human beings bring the mystery of the Son within them and let it grow there. In that way they reverence God, they reverence the Son, they are daughters and sons. "In the Son," we read, "we are sons and daughters."

Being-Human in Listening

The Thou-capacity of the human being has many opportunities for expression. One of the most precious lies in the capacity to listen. One need not "make a big deal" of it or let one's imagination run wild. Anyone knows how beneficial it is to encounter someone who can really listen. Then encounter takes place, and repeated healing as well. Often a psychotherapist's only effective medicine is attentive, alert, and sympathetic listening.

The human being's thou-capacity means, altogether essentially, being free from self and free for others. I remember a cartoon in which a very intoxicated person fumbles his way around an advertising pillar for the hundredth time, crying out in fear, "Help! I'm locked in!" A witty cartoon, but also an apt metaphor for oppressed, I-inebriated persons incapable of saying, of meaning, "thou" — persons who in their myopic state only circle themselves, their needs, their fears, and so on, failing to see that the world around is open and ready for encounter.

The thou-capacity also means leaving others room and making room for their own being. As the saying goes: "Why do you always want to make people different? They're different already!" The reference is to our eager wish to (re)model others in our own image, after our own notions. Here the other can become the simple extension of my own "I." Then encounter is no longer possible. Especially tragic is the thou-incapacity or thou-weakness in a marital or family relationship. Partnership encounter can only take place when I make room, living space, for the actual "thou," the other "I." Max Frisch once put it this way: "After all, love, the wonderful thing about love, consists just in this, that it keeps us on tenterhooks, in readiness to follow someone in all of that person's possible unfolding."

It's also quite essential for the thou-capacity that one keep alive in oneself or enlarge the capacity to listen to one's own being Not a few persons give this answer to the question of when something in their life began to go wrong: "I didn't belong to myself. I heard a still, small movement in myself, a direction, a contact, a warning, and didn't pay any attention to it. I didn't listen to my inner voice. I didn't listen to my feeling that told me that something wasn't right in that relationship."

Persons who cannot be "hearful" and obedient to their true selves, fall prey to persons, fall prey to addictions. Freedom is the capacity to be obedient to oneself. How shattered in their freedom human beings are — in their capacity to be obedient to their true selves — is seen in Paul as the exemplary case, and he says: "I do not do the good I want, but the evil I do not want is what I do" (Rom. 7:19).

Scripture testifies to the spiritual experience that obedience to God bestows actual freedom and protects or rescues us from imprisonment in a fatal dependency upon others and ourselves. The biblical expression, "One must obey God rather than human beings," is not an expression of immaturity, but points the way to freedom. The truth of such a paradox directs our gaze to "great persons," directs our gaze toward Jesus: Jesus was obedient *and* free. There is no freedom without obedience. There is no real obedience without freedom.

The Thou-Capacity in Gift of Self

The person with thou-capacity is the one who can make a gift of self. He or she is the one who has time for..., who is attentive to..., who endorses..., who can set someone free from..., who is reliable.... In these words and phrases we hear the echo of a thousand daily events and experiences. Valid for such persons is Jesus' mighty word, "Those who find their life will lose it, and those who lose their life for my sake will find it" (Matt. 10:39).

Theologian Heinz Zahrndt recounts in one of his books the story of such a surrender of one's own life. A tribe of headhunters had renounced hunting human beings, but only provisionally. After lengthy indecision, the chief, at a great feast, permitted them to kill the first person they would find at night in the woods. The headhunters came upon a man, beat him to death, and only then realized that it was their chief that they had slain. It did not take them long to realize that the chief had done this on purpose. They were utterly shocked and renounced headhunting for good. Still today one can visit the monument to this story on Taiwan.

A powerful, anything but everyday, story. But it is also true that, more frequently than we may be aware, there are persons who, out of their inner freedom, out of love, in dedication to justice, devote their time, their strength, their dignity, even their lives, to others, to one another. On the grand scale and on the small scale this is what keeps the world going.

Even in situations to which we are long since accustomed and which we do not consciously relate to self-giving, obedience, asceticism, and "going beyond ourselves," an inner movement is often at work that has to do with an address to the "thou." What respect for one another is required of the citizens in a democracy if the democracy is to be able to function! Persons who wish to be creative and loyal, although a political party may be in power whose direction and laws work to their disadvantage, must be capable of putting legitimate wishes aside. How much mutual cooperation of minds and hearts is necessary if, in a family, different vacation plans are to be reduced to a common denominator! Democratic, political, and economic cooperation can be realized only when persons are ready to let themselves be "determined," to be "co-determined," and in this sense to be obedient.

When persons in interior freedom are "there" for one another, then they can find a sense and meaning in their lives. Victor Frankl's "logotherapy" relies especially on this experience: life and meaning are to be found in existing-for.

In existing-for one achieves one's own profile. The word "profile" derives from the Latin *pro fila*, "before the line." It designated a soldier who walked out in front of the ranks and did battle or fought a duel, like David and Goliath, instead of all the others.

All the experiences mentioned here can also be linked to the verse in Paul: "Bear one another's burdens, and in this way you will fulfill the law of Christ" (Gal. 6:2).

Being-We as an Expression of the Spiritual Mystery of God

It might be interesting to ask people what they regard as a miracle, how they would describe it and whether they have ever experienced one. Perhaps biblical miracles would be mentioned, or the "wonders of nature," or the wonders of a faith healer. For years I've liked to talk about the "wonder of the we." Behind that lies the experience that it is a miracle for me when a real oneness, a unity, grows between different persons. We all but stand riveted before the alternatives of saying that the little word "we" is a "nonword," a word without meaning — or calling it a miracle word. We say the "we" of a people ("We the people"), the "we" of the church (one Spirit and one Body), the "we" of a friendship ("You and I are one, are a we"). Is this not a miracle, when different beings are one? Is not "we" really a wonder-word?

In view of the Trinitarian mystery of God, one is inclined to see the Holy Spirit, who "proceeds from the Father and the Son," as represented in "we." In the biblical account of creation, God creates through the word and the breath of the "spirit," which wafts over all, and which Yahweh breathes "into [the man's] nostrils," so that it becomes "the breath of life" (see Gen. 2:7). At the creation of the human being, we hear "Let *us* make humankind . . . " (Gen. 1:26). This "us," this plural, has been puzzled over a great deal. Is it a *plurale majestatis*, as with royal monarchs who begin their decrees with the word "We"? Is its meaning that of a linguistic signal for the plenitude of God? May we bring statements of the three-in-oneness of God into connection with it? These questions must be left standing. Biblically,

the working of the Spirit, and thereby the "wonder of the we,"
is especially clear in three phenomena: first, in that of *oneness
and multiplicity*, of which the creation is a mighty expression.
Closely bound up with this is the *witness for truth*. And finally,
again closely bound up with the first two, is the *bipolar oneness
of freedom and law.*

Unity and Multiplicity

In the creation account, the reader is confronted with the biblical
"chaos theory," with the Hebrew *tohu wavohu*, whose equiva-
lent has become proverbial in some languages: in German, we
have *Irrsal und Wirrsal* (Martin Luther's translation, "disorder
and confusion"), corresponding to the English "a formless void"
(Gen. 1:2 — more literally, the earth was "void and empty").
Over the turbulent primal flood wafts God's Spirit, God's breath,
God's breathing. Through the word of Yahweh's breath, through
the word of God's Spirit, reality is realized, and form and life
are shaped. What has been disarray and chaos becomes one, becomes a meaningful shape of cosmos and life. The plenitude and
multiplicity of powers become a whole. Much of the fascination
of crystals and tiny beings, of flowers, beasts, and human beings,
lies precisely in this fact, that an abundance of separate parts is
unified into a wondrous whole. In human generation, when "two
become one flesh," there arises, out of endlessly many different
pieces of information in the woman's egg and the man's seed, a
new being, a new person.

In the most varied ways, the nearness of the Spirit, and of
the process of the unification of the disparate, is made clear in
the New Testament. When in the Annunciation scene Mary is
touched by the Spirit of God, heaven and earth, God and the
human being are united in Christ. From here a trajectory spans
all the way to Jesus' dying: there on Golgotha, hanging on the
cross between heaven and earth, expelled from earth and not yet
received by heaven, Jesus breathes his life, his breath, his spirit
back to God: "Father, into your hands I commend my spirit."

It is impossible to miss the process of unification in the New Testament, especially in the Epistles. At first, after Jesus' death, the disciples scattered, but later, as we read in the Acts of the Apostles, they were in the upper room, "constantly devoting themselves to prayer, together with certain women, including Mary the mother of Jesus" (Acts 1:14). Then, in the event of Pentecost, a new conception occurs: the new community, later called "church," becomes aware of itself, and is elevated to a new step in its development. All were "beside themselves" at the experience of understanding one another: How is it possible that Parthians, Medes, and Elamites, inhabitants of Mesopotamia, Judaea, and Cappadocia (see Acts 2:8–11), despite their varied languages, come together in a community of understanding? "Hearers of the word" (Karl Rahner) are the miracle of unity in multiplicity, the wonder of the "we," of the "I" that encounters itself.

In decisive passages of the New Testament, then, the primitive Christian theology of community sees the wonder of unity in multiplicity through the Holy Spirit. For example, Paul uses the image of the many members of one Body, and speaks of the various gifts, the charisms, and the one Spirit:

> Now there are varieties of gifts, but the same Spirit; and there are varieties of services, but the same Lord; and there are varieties of activities, but it is the same God who activates all of them in every one. To each is given the manifestation of the Spirit for the common good.... For just as the body is one and has many members, and all the members of the body, though many, are one body, so it is with Christ. For in the one Spirit we were all baptized into one body — Jews or Greeks, slaves or free — and we were all made to drink of one Spirit. (1 Cor. 12:4–7, 12–13)

Procreation and Prophetic Witness

The mysterious working of the Spirit, who "wafts where he will," in the Old Testament is especially felt when that Spirit touches human beings and chooses, inspires, enables them to perform prophetic witness in the service of Yahweh. Prophets and prophetesses are "Spirit men," "Spirit women," whose own spirit is awakened and enlightened by God's Spirit. Two of the many passages that could be cited verify this: "When the Spirit rested upon them, they prophesied" (Num. 11:25). "The Spirit of the Lord came upon him, and he judged Israel" (Judg. 3:10).

Testimony and witness are matters of procreation. Only the one impregnated by God can proclaim God. The paragon among all instances is the case of Mary. In a pregnant person who is "expecting," we see God's love incarnate, which then comes through that person into the world. The one who is not really pregnant of God will have to say, "We gave birth only to wind" (Isa. 26:18).

In the New Testament, it is especially the Pentecost event that enables persons to bear witness. If the disciples had at first, "out of fear," hidden "behind bolted doors," now they stepped forth intrepidly and gave witness — even when later they were persecuted, even killed. Christian "freedom of speech" has its origin in this working of the Spirit. The members of the young community are assured that they need not fear when haled into court: the Spirit will instill in them what they should say. The Spirit is the Spirit of candor.

Freedom and Law: The Letter Kills

Freedom and law are seen in the New Testament in an uncommonly sharp tension: "The letter kills, but the Spirit gives life" (2 Cor. 3:6). The Spirit-granted experience of freedom belongs to the bedrock of the Christian experience of faith. But, at the same time, there is always the struggle for a right understanding of law and freedom, since freedom is not intended to be only a "cloak" covering evil. Freedom without law is irresponsible, without direction or measure. Law without freedom means rigidity, compulsion, death. The insoluble tension can be expressed in the saying: "Order doesn't create life, but each life creates its own order."

For the Spirit, who creates life and works from liberty, everything bodily becomes the "free space" of reality and realization.

Being-We and Saying-We in Communication

When persons can really say "we," a peak is attained in the phenomenon of communication. Communication is in the service of we-becoming. The "we" is the fruit of successful communication.

Christian Pluralism — in the Spirit

The Holy Spirit, personally, is the mystery and source of Christian pluralism. After all, the Spirit is the mystery of unity *and* multiplicity, of multiplicity in unity, of unity in multiplicity. There is much to be said for the argument that, for the church of today, there is basically no more important textbook chapter to be learned than that of the Holy Spirit. When the Spirit of Jesus Christ breathes through the church on all levels, it is possible to live multiplicity and unity. Otherwise the church breaks to pieces. With all the different stylistic sensitivities, all the conflicting ideas of moral norms, all the tensions between the "base" and the "hierarchy," the Holy Spirit is the ultimate guarantor of a living unity in multiplicity.

Priests are often described as "servants of unity." This is certainly a crucial service on their part, that is, on the part of all who bear a special pastoral responsibility in the communities. But we can and must add that all who have the responsibility for pastoral work are also servants of multiplicity. The capacity for communication always means, as well, living in the tension between conflict and consensus. In meditating on the New Testament, one finds some seventy passages where conflict and confrontation occur. Many of these confrontations lead to divisions, many lead to a newer, deeper unity. The phrase in the Acts of the Apostles, "They were one heart and one soul," shows only one side of the history of the church. On the reverse side, we read that Christians were in constant conflict and search. The most outstanding symbolic figures for this fruitful confrontation, but also for reconciliation, are Peter and Paul (where the actual antipodes, Paul and James, were the principals, and Peter more the mediator).

Here we see how important the experience of the Spirit is: What prompted the decision to admit the gentiles to the Christian faith without imposing on them the obligations of Jewish belief and practice? In the final analysis it wasn't hairsplitting theological debates, but a vital openness and the experience of the Spirit. Then, when Peter was preaching before the captain Cornelius, together with the latter's friends and relatives:

> The Holy Spirit fell upon all who heard the word. The circumcised believers who had come with Peter were astounded that the gift of the Holy Spirit had been poured out even on the gentiles, for they heard them speaking in tongues and extolling God. Then Peter said, "Can anyone withhold the water for baptizing these people who have received the Holy Spirit just as we have?" So he ordered them to be baptized in the name of Jesus Christ. (Acts 10:44–48)

Witness and Courage

I heard from a Christian of the former Yugoslavia a reflection on giving testimony that might well make us think a bit. He is an engineer and would have been able to get a good position. But he was blocked by the fact that he was not prepared to enter the Communist Party. Acquaintances and friends spoke to him, and said: "You certainly can join the Party. After all, we know what you really think." And he answered, "Yes, I know, and you know, but do my children know too?"

And so it is not a matter of an abstract truth, not of just being "in the truth" oneself, but also of "bearing witness to the truth." Along this path, on the path of witness, truth comes into the world. This holds especially for Jesus as God's witness. But it holds as well for any witness that people bear to the truth. There is a whole spectrum of expressions that have to do with "bearing testimony": go on record as, have the political courage to, come out in favor of, make it clear that, demonstrate that, make a statement to the effect that, cast a vote for. The "silent majority" — or "silent minority," for that matter — is often enough to blame when truth and justice have inadequate room in social, political, and ecclesial life. Witness-bearing can have unpleasant consequences. The most unpleasant may be when we learn that, despite all good intentions, we are on the wrong side. But only on the path of witness is life conceived and transmitted on the level of the Spirit. A capacity for witness means a capacity for the "we." Through their testimony, persons emerge from themselves and make a transition to the "thou," publicly. In witness, they make the offer of encounter.

I-thou-we: In being I-thou-we human encounter and human communication occur. In I-thou-we we can see something of a reflection of the mystery of the triune God. The process will forever remain a mystery. But this mystery of faith in love is granted "that we may have life, and have it more abundantly" (John 10:10) and communicate it to one another.

Chapter 12

Communication in the Context of Culture and Church

Ignatius Loyola and the art of communication — our approach to this theme has been historical. In the course of the exposition, bridges of understanding emerged, leading to the present. In conclusion some areas need to be sketched out in the quest for better communication: the search for successful encounter in the world of today; the church's openness to dialogue; the documents of the Thirty-Fourth General Congregation of the "Jesuit sons of Ignatius"; individual and joint attempts to acquire a proficiency in the art of communication.

The Age of Mass Communication

One of the distinguishing characteristics of our times is surely that we are the "age of the mass media," or of "mass communication." The information flow has become an information flood, to the point that the greatest problem is coming to be the selection of material. Instead of simply learning or learning how to learn, we also have to learn to unlearn, to get rid of useless, out-dated intellectual debris.

Conversations are no longer held only standing at tables in coffee houses, but are organized over the electronic media. E-mail facilitates quick contact all over the world. The media and communications market is booming and creating employment opportunities.

It is possible to imagine a meaningful and livable democracy only under the supposition that a maximal number of persons have access to information and communication, to group thinking and group decision-making. Organizing a campfire chat or other conventional conversation session can be difficult enough; how much more difficult will it be to organize a meaningful communication among many millions of persons, through newspapers, radio, television, the Internet, and so on. The "round table" and the round tables from the days when the Berlin Wall fell, and, later, the fact of German reunification, where what "belongs together" is once more slowly "coming together," show that it is possible to bring partners from the most widely diversified political, social, and religious backgrounds to "one table."

It is no great task to tally up all the deficits of societal mass communication. But over against the factual difficulties in our complex, pluralistic society, it is astonishing how manifold are the positive possibilities of mass media communication. True, new opportunities entail new dangers. In particular, the phenomenon of child pornography on the Internet shows how improved information and communication opportunities can overflow into a marketplace pandering to the human contempt for human beings.

Time spent in front of television or at the computer keyboard takes time away from personal conversation and can degenerate into pseudo-communication. Statistically, a German married couple now spends no more than an average of a few minutes a day in personal conversation. No wonder that the failure to cultivate communication is one of the crucial reasons why relationships collapse.

The point here is not to present either a pessimistic or an optimistic analysis of a culture, but only a graphic outline of the process of communication. Here a somewhat extended passage from the Christmas address of German Federal President Roman Herzog in the year 1997 can serve our purpose. Herzog takes off from the notion that Christmas is "all about messages — and hence about what today is called 'communication.' " And he goes on:

Thank God we live in a society in which freedom reigns, and where no one is told how to develop and evolve personally. This leads inevitably to the formation of groups in our society. But it must not lead to unbridgeable chasms. And so, today more than ever, we need conversation with one another. Conversations loosen up cramped minds, they clarify misunderstandings and build new bridges: people, young and old, need contact and information. Germans and foreigners must speak with each other. Politicians need citizens' experience. Technologists and engineers must ask themselves the questions asked by the concerned lay person. Representatives of diverse cultures must explain their manner of life to one another. And Germans in East and West can still learn a great deal from each other. A rational conversation never begins with the impetus to communicate. It always begins with the readiness and patience to listen.

Understanding, conversation, tolerance: these are decisive cues for our future. Whether we shall solve the problems of the future depends entirely on whether we are able to bring ourselves to accept solutions developed in common and implemented in common. None of us can shape the future alone. Neither can politicians alone ensure the future of pensions, nor can students alone put in place a reform of our education, nor will the future of life be decided only in biomedical labs.

But community and dialogue have an unconditional prerequisite: whether we like it or not, it is necessary that we have trust. In ever more areas, we cannot personally oversee and check what is going on. Nor is trust only a matter between life partners, or between parents and children. We have to trust our physician, our attorney, and the many scientists who contribute to shaping our lives. Politicians know the importance of trust on the part of the citizenry for the functioning of a democracy, and the economy knows, meanwhile, that trust can even be a decisive economic factor.

There is no trust without trustworthiness. Trust needs reliability, and reliability is not won by manipulation and empty rhetoric. It needs a language that can be understood. Platitudes and pretentious jargon inspire no trust. Those who wish to win trust had better be clear in their speech and use convincing arguments. We don't care that experts consider something correct or harmless. We'd like to have some notion of why. (Herzog, 1997, 1321)

Federal President Herzog goes on to mention some successful efforts at encounter. The address itself was a successful attempt to alert many people to the problems and possibilities of communication.

Dialogue as the New Path for the Church

The original formulation was even a bit stronger than this heading. In his encyclical *Ecclesiam Suam*, Pope Paul VI wrote, "Dialogue is a new way to be church" (no. 63). This is not only saying that we should speak with others as a part of a missionary strategy, or that we should only preach to them. Nor do the pope's words merely recommend a new pastoral method. They express something essential in the church's self-understanding. Its very identity means that the church is encounter. Dialogue is the lifeline of the church and the way to transmit the Gospel.

It was not by chance that Paul VI coined the above expression. He was seeking to carry on in a refined and reflective fashion a dialogue that John XXIII had begun with his down-to-earth humanity. It is tragic that, especially through the encyclical *Humanae Vitae* on contraception, this dialogue became all but a caricature of a dialogue open to the world: his isolated decision, against the great majority of a commission that he had himself appointed, and the effects of this decision for Catholics' understanding of authority were a most heavy burden for Paul VI. And yet, his emphasis on the significance of dialogue in his encyclical *Ecclesiam Suam* will remain a part of his place in the history of the church. Perhaps its partial failure shows precisely that, at least sometimes, dialogue is more than a pleasant fireside chat, or an amusing talk show, or a simple communication of the discovery that "My goodness, we all mean the same thing!" If dialogue is a matter of life, then it is also, and to the same extent, a matter of life and death.

In his emphasis on dialogue, Paul VI sought to extend a line of thinking that was of crucial import at Vatican II. First of all, the manner in which John XXIII opened a window to the world and let fresh air in resulted, it is true, in many elements within the church catching a "chill." But the door had been set ajar, and through it dialogue entered the conciliar aula — despite vehement opposition and even shocking attempts at manipulation.

Dialogue and communication are spoken of in not a few places in the conciliar documents. In the Pastoral Constitution on the Church in the Modern World, we find this basic declaration:

> Giving witness and voice to the faith of the whole people of God gathered together by Christ, this Council can provide no more eloquent proof of its solidarity with the entire human family with which it is bound up, as well as its respect and love for that family, than by engaging with it in conversation about these various problems. (*Gaudium et Spes,* no. 3)

"No more eloquent proof...than by engaging with it in conversation." A strong statement!

Paul VI sought to continue dialogue, and, in Part Three of his 1964 encyclical *Ecclesiam Suam,* testified to dialogue as a pathway of the church. "The church makes itself word, message, dialogue!"

An important and often cited text of the Pontifical Commission for Interreligious Dialogue, indicating the various levels of the phenomenon of dialogue, is found in the document *Dialogue and Proclamation* (1991), which presents four kinds of dialogue:

1. The *dialogue of life,* in which persons seek to live together in an open and neighborly atmosphere, inasmuch as they share with one another their joy and sorrow, their human problems and burdens

2. The *dialogue of action,* in which Christians work together with non-Christians for the comprehensive development and liberation of human beings

3. The *dialogue of religious experience,* in which persons rooted in their own religious traditions share their spiritual wealth, for example, with regard to prayer and contemplation, faith and the quest for God or the Absolute

4. The *dialogue of theological exchange,* in which specialists deepen their understanding of their respective religious heritage and learn to appreciate the values of other heritages. (no. 42)

These four levels show that what is at issue in dialogue is not an intellectual conversation, but a manner of free and open encounter. This makes it evident that dialogue is an essential medium for a church that understands itself as community. The most eloquent expression of such an understanding of church is the so-called "*communio* theology," which developed in the aftermath of the Council. For this theology, *communio* — community, relationship — represents a basic way of understanding the church. *Communio* theology adopts the Old Testament and New Testament word "covenant." Covenant means that God is a God of relation, a God who makes his people a partner, a God who has a history with that people, a God who walks with them on a journey. The mystery of the divine Trinity, as it has taken shape in Christian faith, can be summed up as: "God is relation," or, more biblically: "God is love."

These are not anachronistic formulations that have succumbed to the spirit of the twentieth-century church of the Council. They are the bedrock of ecclesiology and theology. To bring it once more to light and influence is the longing of many people in the church. These persons' greatest sorrow is the incapacity for a living community, a partnership, solidarity. A breach of the covenant with God and liquidation of community among human beings are the strongest expressions of what faith understands by sin. Sin means destruction of relationships.

To be sure, an examination of conscience on the part of the church, under the heading of dialogue and communication, shows that it is precisely in these categories that the church's own limits, its mistakes, indeed, its guilt, come to light, in the past and present alike. Speaking of the "methods of intolerance or even constraint in the service of truth," John Paul II writes with reference to a declaration of Vatican II:

> Those painful traits of the past yield a lesson for the future, which must make every Christian hold fast to the Council's golden principle: "Truth has no other claim than that of the truth itself, which gently and yet powerfully permeates the spirit." (*Tertio Millennio Adveniente,* no. 35).

Communication as the "Old Path" of the "New Church"

The image of a church of dialogue, the *communio* church, is not only suitable as a mirror of conscience for the past and the present, which it is first and foremost, but places something of the brilliance of Christian origins before one's eyes: "See how they love one another!" Granted, this brilliance of the church of the origins casts many shadows, too. Granted, the "first Christians" were not always "of one heart and soul" (Acts 4:32). Counting them up carefully, in some seventy passages some thirty-five different situations of conflict are to be found, and among them some that are quite formidable. For example, Jesus chides the disciples for a behavior that is more like that of the "mighty of this world." Paul warns those responsible for the communities to be "co-workers of joy, not lords of the faith." The Corinthians sin when they eat their fill at their worship assemblies, while the poor in the community go hungry. The community does not know whether they should believe that the Lord will definitively return during their lifetime, or whether they must wait a number of generations. The question of excommunication — the question of who belongs to the community of Jesus Christ and who does not — painfully arises. Three levels are decisive for attempts to solve conflicts in primitive Christianity:

1. On a first level, the aim is to *always to relate to Jesus Christ*. Crucial questions include: Is Jesus a liberating, redeeming point of reference for the life of the parties in conflict? Do they open up, ever and again, to the Holy Spirit, through whom "the love of God is poured forth in their hearts"? "Have you prayed again and again until you became inwardly free and peaceful?" might be a corresponding question for us today.

2. A second, very concrete level is that of *conversation*. Here the crucial element is that one, two, or three persons discuss a conflict and remain in conversation about it.

3. The most frequent level appealed to in the New Testament is the level of *interior dispositions* that have to do with the working of the Spirit. Gerhard Lohfink, in his *Wie hat Jesus Gemeinde gewollt?* (How has Jesus willed community? 116–17), has collected the passages in Scripture in which there is explicit question of togetherness among Christians. These loci attest to the attentiveness of the first Christians to elements of reciprocal relationship: encouragement of one another in faith (Rom. 1:12); recognizing the identity of all as members of the one body of Christ, who belong together (Rom. 12:5); dealing with one another with affection and reverence (Rom. 12:10); seeking unanimity (Rom. 12:16); loving one another (Rom. 13:8); striving for what serves for peace and edification with one another (Rom. 14:19); welcoming one another (Rom. 15:7); instructing one another (Rom. 15:14); greeting one another with a holy kiss (Rom. 16:16); waiting for one another (1 Cor. 11:33); caring for one another (1 Cor. 12:25); serving one another in love (Gal. 5:13); bearing one another's burdens (Gal. 6:2); consoling one another, edifying one another (1 Thess. 5:11); living with one another in

peace (1 Thess. 5:13); bearing with one another in love (Eph. 4:2); speaking the truth to one another (Eph. 4:25); being bound together as members of one body (Eph. 4:25); being good to one another (Eph. 4:32); showing one another mercy (Eph. 4:32); forgiving one another (Eph. 4:32); submitting to one another (Eph. 5:21); respecting one another as superior to oneself (Phil. 2:3); forgiving one another (Col. 3:13); becoming rich in love for one another (1 Thess. 3:12); attending to one another (Heb. 10:24); confessing one's sins to one another (James 5:16); praying for one another (James 5:16); loving one another from the heart (1 Pet. 1:22); being hospitable to one another (1 Pet. 4:9); meeting one another in humility (1 Pet. 5:5); having community with one another (1 John 1:7); loving one another (1 John 3:11, 23; 4:7, 11, 12; 2 John 5).

It would not be the worst exercise in Christian *communio* and communication to complement this list with one's own ideas, make a list of priorities, get going with observation and practice in company with others. This could lead in the direction of a pastoral practice in communication, of which we occasionally hear nowadays, which is supposed to create a network within the community's pastoral activity, and even go beyond it. In this way, we could practice a little of what was set in motion at the beginning of the 1990s under the heading "Dialogue instead of Refusal of Dialogue: How is One to Deal with Others in the Church?" at the behest of the Central Commission of German Catholics, as a dialogue project with major participation on the part of the people of the church.

Perhaps then the introduction from a lecture given by Bishop Hermann Josef Spital (Trier) will prove to be fruitful, and not just strange and foreign sounding.

The title of my lecture, "Jesus Christus, Communicator Perfectus" (Jesus Christ, the Perfect Communicator), which is borrowed from the papal document *Communio et Progressio,* surely has an unusual sound: the German edition translates this: "Christ showed himself a 'Master of Communication.'" But I hope to be able to show that the outlook addressed with this title opens fertile perspectives.

Applying this to the church, Spital formulates: "The church is subject, the locus, content, and goal of the communicative behavior of Jesus Christ in the Holy Spirit."

Jesuits Today and the "Practice of Dialogue"

"Today we understand this clearly...." On what are the Jesuits of the Thirty-Fourth General Congregation, held in 1995, clear and unanimous? The answer is given in a text occasionally called "the song" during this General Congregation:

> No service to the *faith* without fostering justice, without inculturation, without openness to other religious experiences.
> No call to *justice* without sharing faith, without transforming cultures, without cooperation with other traditions.
> No *inculturation* without conversation about faith, without entering into dialogue with other traditions, without making a commitment to justice.
> No *dialogue* without sharing faith with others, without exploring cultures, without a concern for justice. (GK, 408)

One might be of the opinion that it is difficult to find the right melody for this text, to make a song of it. One could think: Here the Jesuits are making an enormous demand on themselves and others. In any case, it is clear that, for the Jesuit profile, the four words, "faith," "justice," "culture," and "dialogue" have been basic words for years, and will remain such in the future.

In what follows, we shall cite certain prominent statements from the "Decree on Interreligious Dialogue." True, the first addressees are Jesuits, and persons sympathetic to Ignatian spirituality. Still, the message of the documents could certainly be of inspiring importance for others.

To begin, the General Congregation encourages "all Jesuits" to "overcome prejudices and preconceptions, be they historical, cultural, social, or theological, and with their whole heart to work together with all persons of good will, in order to foster peace, justice, harmony, human rights, and respect for all of God's creation. This must especially occur through dialogue" (GK, 431–32).

As the font and source of this dialogue, a theological declaration sees God's dialogue with human beings. "We acknowledge that God, who wills redemption for all, is leading believers of all religions along paths known only to him, for the harmony of the Reign of God. God's Spirit is with them, in constant dialogue. . . . An open and honest interreligious dialogue is our way of cooperating in God's continuing dialogue with humanity" (GK, 434).

Open dialogue, fertile dialogue, is possible only to the extent that one's own identity, one's own reality, becomes more profoundly grasped and introduced into the dialogue. "True dialogue with believers of other religions requires that we deepen our own Christian faith and our own commitment, since true dialogue takes place only among those rooted in their own identity" (GK, 437).

At the end of the decree, the final conclusion is drawn:

> The Jesuit legacy of creative response to the call of the Spirit in concrete life situations is a motive for the development of a culture of dialogue in our encounters with believers of other religions. This culture of dialogue must become a specific mark of our Society, which is sent forth to the whole world to work for the greater glory of God and to help human beings. (GK, 442)

The formulation, "the Jesuit legacy of creative response," after all that we have said about the Ignatian art of communication, can be regarded neither as an invention of the twentieth century, nor as sheer arrogance, but rather as the "creative recall" of an origin pregnant with the future. Even more than the memory of marketplace preacher Pater Leppich or Mario von Galli of the mighty gestures and words, the declarations of the General Congregation can be a witness to, and the goal for, a self-imposed obligation to communicate. This duty is more easily set down in a document than lived every day.

Summing Up:
The Rules of the Game

There are various ways to sum up a book and its messages. Here an attempt will be made to do so by summarizing some of the rules of the game.

The governing notion is simple. Communication is a process of sharing-in, of sharing-with, of mutual giving and taking. Our entire life consists in an interplay of sharing-in and sharing-with. The better this goes, the more successful our life is. There is even, in our life, a happiness, which the Bible calls "blessedness," that is possible even in "unhappy" situations.

The first and basic rules for communication in human life may be stated as follows.

Be conscious of your way of communicating.

Those wishing to grow in their conduct of communication will find it important to become profoundly cognizant of the way in which, for good or ill, they deal with persons. Here they may ask: How do I experience myself? Do I have "communication fears"? Am I more reticent, or am I more voluble? Do I have secret premises that guide my feeling and relating, and so on?

Develop your manner of communication
in communication with others.

Instead of simply planning a more positive relationship of communication in our heads, the thing to do is to test this out in direct communication with others. Here, questions like the following can be helpful. What strikes you in my manner of encounter, of conversation, of communicating? How do you "experience me" in my exchanges with you and with others? What is helpful? What disturbs you? What would you wish for me — and yourself? Could you provide me with a bit of "development help for my self-help"?

Practice the art of communication.

There is only one path from knowing something to being able to do it: practice. When you are in a situation calling for communication, when you have discovered a weakness in communication, or a new opportunity, turn this into an "exercise." Take a while with it. Be attentive to the exercise. Look back, and, if possible, talk it over with a friend.

First practice listening.

The art of communication begins with exercise in listening. Ask yourself repeatedly: Am I with the other, his or her message, feelings, willing, or do I usually just spin around on the axis of my own wishes, intentions, feelings?

Take the liberty of asking questions.

Asking questions in a conversation shows your interest in the other and in that person's message. There is a saying, "One who asks is dumb. One who doesn't ask stays dumb!" Those who have experience here can even say: Asking is itself the beginning of wisdom! Unexplained misunderstandings weigh communication down. So ask. Don't "drill" the other (especially don't "drill through" the other), but open the other up with questions, even if you have to turn the question key more than once.

Work on, and with, language.

Just as you lay out tools for a job you plan to do, or get things ready for a chess game or soccer match, so you have to refine the tool of language. Learn helpful figures of speech from others. Try some yourself, and see what helps and what does not.

Give the necessary information, and speak with those involved.

It is possible to give superfluous information. The rule to give the necessary information will look like such a superfluous rule. "Of course I knew that!" we might hear. But it is too little observed. It is astonishing how many "sins" are committed against this rule. A person finds out that her job description has been changed without prior agreement. It happens all the time: the people most affected by something are not consulted about it, only a few "gray eminences." If something immediately concerns someone, that person must be promptly spoken to or provided with the relevant information. We can save ourselves a great deal of time and energy making good the omissions at a later date.

Use the power of praise and apology, please and thank you.

Praise and apology, please and thank you, are the basis of a good relationship. Recognition of another does not make me smaller. Nor does an apology, when one has done something wrong or wounded someone. Thanking someone does not knock a little point off your crown, and saying please at least gives you a chance of getting what you ask for.

Believe in the "treasure hidden in the field" of the other.

The basis of all real human communication is believing in the mystery of the other persons, in their dignity, in their uniqueness, in the value of their lives, in their freedom, even if the preciousness of a life may be very hard to see, or we ourselves may be shortsighted. Respect for another — and for myself! — is communication's meat and drink. This is something that bears conscious repetition in my own mind.

Stand by your communication weaknesses.

Even after a hundred courses in communication, people will still rub one another the wrong way, will still misunderstand one another in an encounter. A refusal to learn to live with this makes everything even more difficult. Consideration and forbearance with regard to one's own communication weaknesses and those of others is one of the "basics" when it comes to dealing with one another. Perfectionism can be lethal. Anyone who communicates makes many mistakes. Anyone who does not communicate, makes only one — not living in encounter. Is the choice difficult?

Be honest, authentic, and realistic.

The reverse test shows that nothing disturbs and destroys communication as much as lying, untruthfulness, excuses, insincerity. These create an atmosphere of mistrust. Not only do lies have short legs, they are the gravediggers of encounter.

A major lie, being an intentionally false statement, can be seen when it twists and conceals a person in his or her very essence. Communication means seeking increasingly deeper contact with reality through mutual exchange. Who am I? Who are you? What is at issue? What are the prospects? What are the possibilities?

Rules for Wrecking Communication

We occasionally hear soccer fans discuss a new rule: Is the game more exciting when it is decided by the "sudden death" goal? What should be punished as a foul? In other words, there are rules that make a game go more smoothly, and there are others that slow it down and mess it up. It's the same with communication. If you hold to certain rules, you can greatly increase the probability that a conversation will go wrong. In the spirit of C. S. Lewis's *Screwtape Letters,* here are some rules for bedeviling a conversation, for wrecking an encounter.

- *Dominate the conversation* with your experiences, anecdotes, ideas, and so on, and allow the others to express themselves as little as possible.

- Come on as *the greatest possible know-it-all,* an unimpeachable authority. Be an "Ipse dixit" (He himself hath spoken).

- *Interrupt* others as often as possible.

- Be *condescending,* and let others feel that you regard them as incompetent.

- Get yourself a collection of "killer phrases," like, "As everyone has known for a long time,... " "Only you and your party can be so pig-headed and blind." "Things were never that way."

- Lower your voice and carry on an annoying private conversation with your neighbor.

- Exploit the *irritating effect of nonverbal interventions* like disdainfully smiling, wrinkling your brow with skepticism during others' contributions, and so on.

- *Interpret* others: "Of course you mean,... " instead of asking them what they mean with their statement, or asking them to be more exact in their explanation or comments.

- Speak as *generally as possible,* using "everybody" instead of "I," and keep your remarks as general and abstract as possible.

- Make it understood that you regard "this kind of conversation" as nothing but a *waste of time,* and avoid contributing anything positive to the conversation yourself.

- Keep bringing up *points of order*, so that there can be no substantive debate on anything.

"Please Don't . . . " and "Yes, Thank You!"

In a course with some fifty sisters at the Institut Regina Mundi in Rome, I once collected reactions to these two questions: "What, in my experience, can work to *block a conversation?*" and, "What, in my experience, can *further a conversation?*" Multiplying the number of sisters by their average age, you might call the answers to these two questions the collected wisdom of some 2,500 years of life. If we will, then, we can learn something from these answers, or at least recognize ourselves in many of them. What is ultimately at stake Alfred Delp, S.J., once described in one sentence: "Personal dialogue is the basic form of mental vitality."

Please don't go away if you're here for me.

- Don't say, "I have time for you," and then keep looking at your watch.

- Don't say, "We must definitely talk about this sometime," and then keep putting off the conversation.

- Don't say, "That's very interesting to me!" when it takes you a scant five minutes to signal your lack of interest.

- Speak with me more than about me.

Please don't take me lightly.

- Don't take me just as a "case."

- Don't say, "Oh, that's not so bad!" and belittle my problem or my guilt.

- Don't say, "Our little problem child, what is it this time?"

- Don't try to encourage me with childish joking.

- Don't treat me like an unruly child.

- Don't keep interrupting me in mid-sentence.

- Be careful with, "You only need to...."

Please don't judge me.

- Don't compare me with others: "Just look at,...how she...!"

- Don't keep showing me the contradictions in my behavior. I already know my inconsistencies, and they hurt.

- Don't say, "You're a hopeless case."

- Don't always be warning me, and don't berate me. Don't tell me, "You sound just like my mother."

- Don't threaten me.

- Don't "grade" my behavior and speech.

Please don't act like royalty.

- Don't speak like a teacher to his students. That blocks me.

- Don't present me with "done decisions," but give me aids to make my own decisions.

- Don't tie me to you.

- Don't drill me when you sense that I would not like to talk about something, or not yet.

- Don't require of me what I cannot manage as yet.

- Don't always be telling me how everything is just fine with you.

- Don't give me the feeling that you see right through me.

- Don't tell anyone what I tell you; otherwise I can't talk with you anymore.

Thank you for accepting me as I am.

- For not making me afraid to show you my weaknesses.
- For showing that you hold me in high regard.
- For accepting me with my shortcomings.
- For showing me that you like me.
- For seeing, behind all of my failings, a child of God.

Thank you for understanding me.

- For your understanding sympathy in your reactions.
- For really listening to me.
- For asking me understanding, empathetic questions.
- For helping me to sort out what's been said.
- For helping me to understand myself better.

Thank you for taking me seriously.

- For treating me as an adult person.
- For showing genuine interest in me.
- For not playing the great savior.
- For letting me give you something too.

Thank you for encountering me without prejudices.

- For not lining up everything automatically into a fixed picture of me.

- For not categorizing me as the "quiet type," the "cheerful type," the "difficult type," the "depressed type," and so on.
- For judging, but not with your nose in the air.
- For permitting me to be a mystery.

Thank you for leaving me my freedom.

- For not putting me under time pressure.
- For not creating an atmosphere that puts me under pressure to express myself.
- For having so much patience with me.

Thank you for walking the way of truth with me.

- For lovingly holding me to the truth.
- For making me aware of attempts to run away from something.
- For giving me meaningful feedback.
- For allowing me to hope, and for honestly confronting me.
- For mirroring what I say, feel, and think.
- For letting the way of truth issue in the Sacrament of Reconciliation.

Thank you for being you.

- For feeling with me, but not breaking down under my burden.
- For being not a simple echo, but a conversation partner.
- For paying attention to yourself, as well, and your limits and needs.

Thank you for encouraging me.

- For questioning my despair, and showing me that the burden of proof lies with despair.

- For asking, "And what is the good part of the problem?"

- For having confidence, in my regard, that "for those who love God, all things work together unto good."

Thank you for giving me good advice.

- For giving me advice, but not cut-and-dried advice.

- For indicating choices, and letting me choose among them.

- For advising me always to express my situation in writing.

- For counseling me, but without playing the know-it-all or reciting only your experiences and solutions.

Thank you for being a person of faith.

- For helping me to trust.

- For supporting me with your prayer.

- For helping me to pray.

- For laying your hand on me in prayer.

- For asking me, "Can you give thanks for the difficulty you are in?"

- For helping me to leave room open for God.

The Sun of Friendship

This list, the product of so many experiences lived and struggled through, in failure and success, tells us that it is sensible and helpful to know rules of communication, and to refer to them, so that human life together can take a more "philanthropic" and "beatifying" form. But it is just as clear that it is only on the path of experience, the path of learning through trial and error, that the "art of communication" can be discovered. It is a step-by-step process. But the "art" is never without a sense of being surprised and "gifted" in a communicating relationship. Those favored, those "gifted," who open themselves to encounter, often experience the gift of friendship as well. Jesus speaks of this friendship to those who have gone his way with him through all of its difficulties, and to whom he has revealed everything that he could convey that he has received from the heart of God: "I have called you friends, because I have made known to you everything that I have heard from my Father" (John 15:15).

One of those who walked the way of life in the footsteps of Jesus, one of the "friends in the Lord" and friends of Ignatius Loyola, Peter Canisius, says, in a sermon on the gift of friendship:

Since one does not live without friends, and to remove friendship would mean nothing else but to deprive the world of the sun, so will I take all necessary means to make a sincere friend, as David found in Jonathan and Paul in Timothy — a friend who is another "I," a judicious admonitor, experienced physician, and magnanimous moral judge.

Bibliography

Frequently Cited Works and Basic Texts, with Abbreviations

BC   Ignatius of Loyola. *Beiträge zu seinem Charakterbild* (Contributions to his profile). Cologne, 1932.

BDP   Ignatius of Loyola. *Der Bericht des Pilgers* (Pilgrim's report). Trans. and ed. Burkhart Schneider. 3d. ed. Freiburg im Breisgau, 1977. In English see *The Autobiography of St. Ignatius Loyola, with Related Documents.* Ed. John C. Olin. Trans. Joseph F. O'Callaghan. New York: Fordham University Press, 1993.

BU   Ignatius of Loyola. *Briefe und Unterweisungen* (Letters and instructions). Ed. and trans. Peter Knauer. Würzburg, 1993. In English see *Letters of Ignatius of Loyola.* Chicago: Loyola University Press, 1959, and *Counsels for Jesuits: Selected Letters and Instructions of Saint Ignatius Loyola.* Ed. Joseph N. Tylenda. Chicago: Loyola University Press, 1985.

GB   Ignatius of Loyola. *Geistliche Briefe* (Spiritual letters). Introduction by Hugo Rahner. Einsiedeln, 1956.

GGJ   Ignatius of Loyola. *Gründungstexte der Gesellschaft Jesu* (Foundational texts of the Society of Jesus). Ed. and trans. Peter Knauer. Würzburg, 1998.

GK   *Dekrete der 31.-34. Generalkongregation der Gesellschaft Jesu* (Decrees of the 31st–34th General Congregations of the Society of Jesus). Munich, 1997.

GT   Ignatius of Loyola. *Das geistliche Tagebuch* (*The spiritual diary*). Ed. Adolf Haas and Peter Knauer. Freiburg im Breisgau, 1961. In English see St. Ignatius of Loyola. *Personal Writings.* Trans. Joseph A. Munitiz. New York: Viking Penguin, 1996.

GU   Ignatius of Loyola. *Geistliche Übungen* (Spiritual Exercises). Ed and trans. Peter Knauer. Würzburg, 1998. (Cf. Ignatius von Loyola, *Geistliche Übungen und erläuternde Texte* (Spiritual Exercises and explanatory texts). Ed. Peter Knauer. Leipzig, 1978). In English see *Ignatius of Loyola: The Spiritual Exercises and Selected Works*. Classics of Western Spirituality. Ed. George E. Ganss, Parmananda R. Divarkar, and Edward J. Malatesta. New York: Paulist, 1991.

MEVI   Luis Gonçalves da Câmara. *Memoriale: Erinnerungen an unseren Vater Ignatius* (Memoriale: Memories of Our Father Ignatius). Ed. Peter Knauer. Frankfurt, 1988. In English see *St. Ignatius' Own Story, as Told to Luis González de Cámara, with a Sampling of His Letters*. Trans. William J. Young. Chicago: Regnery, 1956. See also *A Pilgrim's Testament: The Memoirs of St. Ignatius of Loyola, as transcribed by Luís Gonçalves da Câmara*. Trans. Parmananda R. Divarkar. St. Louis: Institute of Jesuit Sources, 1995.

SGJ   *Satzungen der Gesellschaft Jesu und ergänzende Normen*. Munich, 1997. (Numerals refer to the part with the statues and articles.)

TW   Ignatius of Loyola. *Trost and Weisung* (Consolation and instruction). 2d ed. Ed. Hugo Rahner and Paul Imhof. Zurich, 1978.

Other Works

Canisius, Peter. *Briefe* (Letters). Ed. Burkhart Schneider. Salzburg, 1958.

Delp, Alfred. *Gesammelte Schriften* (Collected Works) vol. 4. Ed. Roman Bleistein. Frankfurt, 1984.

Faber, Peter. *Memoriale*. Ed. P. Henrici. Einsiedeln, 1989.

Geiselhart, Helmut. *Das Management-Modell der Jesuiten* (The management model of the Jesuits). Wiesbaden, 1997.

Herzog, Roman. Bulletin No. 110, Bonn 28. December 1995. Christmas Address. Federal Office of Press and Information.

———. Bulletin No. 103, S. 1321, Bonn, 29. December 1997. Christmas Address. Federal Office of Press and Information.

John Paul II. *Tertio millennio adveniente*. November 10, 1994.

Lambert, Willi. *Aus Liebe zur Wirklichkeit: Grundworte ignatianischer Spiritualität* (Out of love for reality: Basic words of Ignatian spirituality). 4th ed. Mainz, 1998.

———. Lambert, Willi. *Beten im Pulsschlag des Lebens: Gottsuche mit Ignatius von Loyola* (Praying in rhythm with life: Seeking God with Ignatius Loyola). 2d ed. Freiburg im Breisgau, 1998.

Lohfink, Gerhard. *Wie hat Jesus Gemeinde gewollt?* Freiburg im Breisgau, 1982, 1993. English trans.: *Jesus and Community: The Social Dimension of Christian Faith.* Trans. John P. Galvin. Philadelphia: Fortress Press, and New York: Paulist Press, 1984.

Nadal, Hieronymus. *Über die Gnade des Gebetes in der Gesellschaft Jesu: Mitteilungen aus den deutschen Provinzen Nr. 103* (The grace of prayer in the Society of Jesus: Communication from the German Provinces). 1935.

O'Malley, John W. *Die ersten Jesuiten.* Trans. K. Mertes. Würzburg, 1995. English original: *The First Jesuits.* Cambridge, Mass.: Harvard University Press, 1993.

Pontifical Council for Interreligious Dialogue, Congregation for the Evangelization of Peoples. *Dialogue and Proclamation.* May 19, 1991.

Paul VI. *Ecclesiam Suam.* August 6, 1964.

Rivera, José R. de. *Kommunikationsstrukturen in den geistlichen Exerzitien des Ignatius von Loyola* (Structures of communication in the Spiritual Exercises of Ignatius Loyola). Hamburg, 1978.

Schavan, Annette. *Dialog statt Dialogverweigerung: Impulse für eine zukunftsfähige Kirche* (Dialogue instead of refusal of dialogue: Thrusts for a Church to the measure of the future). Kevelaer, 1994.

Spee, Friedrich. *Güldenes Tugend-Buch* (Golden book of virtues). Einsiedeln, 1991.

Stich, Helmut. *Kernstrukturen menschlicher Begegnung* (Core structures of human encounter). Munich, 1977.

Teilhard de Chardin, Pierre. *Das göttliche Milieu.* Olten, 1969. In English see *The Divine Milieu.* New York: HarperCollins, 1989.

Tellechea, Ignacio. *Ignatius von Loyola: Allein und zu Fuß* (Ignatius Loyola: Alone and on foot). 2d ed. Zurich, 1995. In English see Ignacio Tellechea. *Ignatius of Loyola: The Pilgrim Saint.* Trans. Cornelius Michael Buckley. Chicago: Loyola University Press, 1994.

Watzlawick, Paul. *Anleitung zum Unglücklichsein* (Instructions for being unhappy). Munich, 1983.

Wilkens, Gerard Th. A. "Unterwegs zum Orden" (On the way to the Order). Dissertation. Munster, 1976.